Number 122
Summer 2009

New Directions fo

Sandra Mathison
Editor-in-Chief

WITHDRAWAL

Environmental Program and Policy Evaluation: Addressing Methodological Challenges

Matthew Birnbaum
Per Mickwitz
Editors

Environmental Program and Policy Evaluation: Addressing
Methodological Challenges
Matthew Birnbaum, Per Mickwitz (eds.)
New Directions for Evaluation, no. 122
Sandra Mathison, Editor-in-Chief

Microfilm copies of issues and articles are available in 16mm and 35mm,
as well as microfiche in 105mm, through University Microfilms Inc., 300
North Zeeb Road, Ann Arbor, Michigan 48106-1346.

New Directions for Evaluation is indexed in Cambridge Scientific Abstracts
(CSA/CIG), Contents Pages in Education (T & F), Educational Research
Abstracts Online (T & F), ERIC Database (Education Resources
Information Center), Higher Education Abstracts (Claremont Graduate
University), Social Services Abstracts (CSA/CIG), Sociological Abstracts
(CSA/CIG), and Worldwide Political Sciences Abstracts (CSA/CIG).

NEW DIRECTIONS FOR EVALUATION (ISSN 1097-6736, electronic ISSN
1534-875X) is part of The Jossey-Bass Education Series and is published
quarterly by Wiley Subscription Services, Inc., A Wiley Company, at
Jossey-Bass, 989 Market Street, San Francisco, California 94103-1741.

SUBSCRIPTIONS cost $85 for U.S./Canada/Mexico; $109 international.
For institutions, agencies, and libraries, $235 U.S.; $275 Canada/Mexico;
$309 international. Prices subject to change.

EDITORIAL CORRESPONDENCE should be addressed to the Editor-in-Chief,
Sandra Mathison, University of British Columbia, 2125 Main Mall,
Vancouver, BC V6T 1Z4, Canada.

www.josseybass.com

Editorial Policy and Procedures

New Directions for Evaluation, a quarterly sourcebook, is an official publication of the American Evaluation Association. The journal publishes empirical, methodological, and theoretical works on all aspects of evaluation. A reflective approach to evaluation is an essential strand to be woven through every issue. The editors encourage issues that have one of three foci: (1) craft issues that present approaches, methods, or techniques that can be applied in evaluation practice, such as the use of templates, case studies, or survey research; (2) professional issues that present topics of import for the field of evaluation, such as utilization of evaluation or locus of evaluation capacity; (3) societal issues that draw out the implications of intellectual, social, or cultural developments for the field of evaluation, such as the women's movement, communitarianism, or multiculturalism. A wide range of substantive domains is appropriate for *New Directions for Evaluation;* however, the domains must be of interest to a large audience within the field of evaluation. We encourage a diversity of perspectives and experiences within each issue, as well as creative bridges between evaluation and other sectors of our collective lives.

The editors do not consider or publish unsolicited single manuscripts. Each issue of the journal is devoted to a single topic, with contributions solicited, organized, reviewed, and edited by a guest editor. Issues may take any of several forms, such as a series of related chapters, a debate, or a long article followed by brief critical commentaries. In all cases, the proposals must follow a specific format, which can be obtained from the editor-in-chief. These proposals are sent to members of the editorial board and to relevant substantive experts for peer review. The process may result in acceptance, a recommendation to revise and resubmit, or rejection. However, the editors are committed to working constructively with potential guest editors to help them develop acceptable proposals.

Sandra Mathison, Editor-in-Chief
University of British Columbia
2125 Main Mall
Vancouver, BC V6T 1Z4
CANADA
e-mail: nde@eval.org

CONTENTS

and methods for evaluating effectiveness should be informed by considering (1) the subject matter of evaluation; (2) available resources and data; (3) scale, scope, and timeframe of the evaluation; and (4) risks.

EDITORS' NOTES

Evaluation has come relatively late to the environmental arena. Now that the environmental field has begun to embrace evaluation, it is increasingly evident that the common denominator across evaluations is complexity. There is complexity in the environmental problems, in the programs and policies that have emerged to address the problems, and in the evaluation responses. Some challenges concern methodology; issues of time horizons, scale, data credibility, and research designs and counter-factuals all need to be better addressed. This issue of *New Directions in Evaluation* addresses these methodological factors.

Complex Environmental Problems

Hardin (1968) wrote in a seminal paper:

> Picture a pasture open to all. It is to be expected that each herdsman will try to keep as many cattle as possible on the commons. . . . The rational herds-man concludes that the only sensible course for him to pursue is add another animal to his herd. And another; and another. . . . But this is the conclusion reached by every rational herdsman sharing the commons. Therein is the tragedy. Each man is locked into a system that compels him to increase his herd without limit—in a world that is limited. (p. 1244)

Environmental problems are frequently more complex than the example cited by Hardin. This makes their management difficult. Thus the problem of overexploitation of natural resources often emerges because inappropriate rules and institutions create incentives that result in unsustainable outcomes (Ostrom, 1990). The problems are made more complex because the full value of a resource is frequently not recognized until long after it has been extracted, processed, and consumed. The common-property nature of many environmental resources aggravates the problem.

Complex Decision Making

Permanent solutions to environmental problems are rare partly due to the "dynamic complexity" of the problems (Senge, 1990; Kakoyannis, 2004). Numerous interacting variables end up compounded on multiple parties with differing values, operating under a high degree of scientific uncertainty (Mickwitz, 2003). The problem of inadequate information is critical because

NEW DIRECTIONS FOR EVALUATION, no. 122, Summer 2009 © Wiley Periodicals, Inc. and the American Evaluation Association. Published online in Wiley InterScience (www.interscience.wiley.com) • DOI: 10.1002/ev.290

1

environmental decision making is often done around "wicked problems" (Rittel & Webber, 1973; Wildavsky, 1979). These problems are too complex to be understood in whole. As one aspect is addressed through framing the problem one way, another layer surfaces. Arguments are made for "comprehensive rational analysis," but the systems are too complex, and at best policy making can evolve only incrementally. At worst, ideology, interest, and institutional behavior take precedent (Weiss, 1995), at times exacerbating the magnitude of the environmental problem. For example, consider the issue of fire suppression. People have different values about fire. Attempts are often made to suppress a fire so as to protect personal assets, most significantly people's homes. However, our history of fire suppression has led to an increase in forest fuels, corresponding to an increase in catastrophic crown fires (Kakoyannis, 2004).

Environmental decision makers have to take into account risks, uncertainties, and ignorance (Wynne, 1992). For instance, consider the well-known example of dichlorodiphenyltrichloroethane (DDT). As described by Hoffmann-Riem and Wynne (2002, p. 123), the science was rigorous enough to establish that this chemical treatment could effectively eradicate mosquito-borne diseases such as malaria. However, it was not known until much later that widespread application of this chemical also harmed many other species. Although risks can be better assessed through more research, uncertainties and ignorance cannot be eliminated from environmental decision making.

Complexity of Evaluation

Despite the diversity of environmental problems, all involve human use of natural resources. Evaluations need to be broad to encompass the full range of environmental, economic, and social impacts (intended and unintended) of environmental policies and programs. Simultaneously, they need to be deep in order to permit insight as to what actually is causing which changes in complex systems. To address the complexity associated with environmental problems, environmental evaluations require individuals possessing a diverse combination of knowledge, skills, experiences, and approaches. It requires building the social capital of various types of experts committed to nurturing a community of savvy evaluators. Environmental program evaluation is a nascent field and is the focus of the methodological challenges discussed in this chapter. One specific challenge raised for evaluators working in the environmental arena concerns the complexity of the systems. Evaluation, when it is done at all, is frequently susceptible to "black box" design. Frequently efforts are made by those with expertise in the natural sciences to identify broad strategies (e.g., education and eco-labeling) targeted at ecological outcomes (such as protection of dolphins) with inadequate attention to the middle part of the equation, where theories of change depend on distinct influences on human behavior that do not result simply from acquisition of new knowledge and attitudes. Similarly, social scientists can construct complex chains in altering human behavior but often infer them to theories with overly simplistic representations of environmental and ecological processes.

Evaluation has taken root in the environmental and conservation community over the past decade. This has largely been due to demands from public and private funders for greater accountability of outcomes arising from the spending of finite funds (see, for instance, Poister, 2003). The evaluators of environmental policies and programs who are responding to this demand (as well as the potential users of the evaluations and those whose efforts are being evaluated) represent a diverse set of disciplines and professional paths. This is probably true in all fields in evaluation. What makes the environmental arena notable is that addressing environmental problems requires practitioners with the ability to focus on changing human behavior while working synergistically with practitioners focused on direct changes to environmental conditions (modifying streams, planting trees). The evaluator in the environmental arena is someone who can encourage these groups to collaborate and see the interconnections between their respective contributions to solving an environmental problem. The need to bring together individuals who understand the human and ecological dimensions of environmental problems creates major challenges for evaluation practice.

The contributors to this issue represent the diversity of perspectives necessary to advance the current state of environmental evaluation. Some authors have a background in the natural sciences, others in the social sciences. Some work in academia; others are in the public sector, and still others come from the nonprofit and private sectors. About half of the authors work exclusively with conservation and biodiversity issues, while others work on pollution control or other environmental issues. Because of their differing traditions and perspectives, there is some variation in terminology. For example, some write of "outcome evaluation," which for others implies "impact evaluation" in referring to the same concept.

Focus on Methodological Challenges

The genesis of this issue of *New Directions for Evaluation* is the first three annual forums of the Environmental Evaluators Network. This entity was established in the United States in 2006 through a U.S. Environmental Protection Agency and National Fish and Wildlife Foundation collaboration. The aim has been to complement AEA's Environmental Topical Interest Group in advancing the field of evaluation in the environmental arena. One prominent theme at the outset was that evaluators practicing in this field struggle with addressing specific methodological challenges. Consequently, this issue is organized around four key methodological challenges and their potential solutions:

1. Differing and frequently long time horizons
2. Disparities in scaling

3. Data quality and credibility issues
4. The problem of research designs for assessing attribution in environmental policies and programs

Each challenge is discussed by two authors to reflect differing perspectives.

Time Horizons. Evaluators have to bridge the gap between the differing time horizons needed to observe change in natural and social systems. Evaluators are expected to assess the impact of short-term policies and programs on environmental outcomes that may take decades to be revealed. Many environmental problems span decades (and, in some instances, as with nuclear waste, millennia). By contrast, public policy and program funding cycles are generally short-term. Scientists build models projecting changes in environmental media—such as air or water—over eons; practitioners and funders wrangle over day-to-day operational issues.

The first perspective on how to evaluate efforts that span contrasting time horizons is given in Chapter 1 by Mikael Hildén, from the Finnish Environment Institute. He looks at adaptive evaluation approaches that direct attention for prospective evaluations to move backward in time and retrospective evaluations to move forward in time. Raymond Gullison and Jared Hardner, two independent consultants, in Chapter 2 introduce a "limiting factor methodology" for addressing situations where the capacity of on-the-ground environmental practitioners is limited to the short run, but where improvements in the natural environment require much longer periods of time to be observed.

Scaling. Environmental problems typically take place across numerous spatial scales, and this creates particular challenges for evaluation—especially in matching the scale of political jurisdiction with that of an ecosystem. For instance, greenhouse gas emissions affect the climate globally although they are produced locally. Clear cutting a forest causes degradation at site-specific habitats. Forest and land use, however, is frequently linked to global demands for timber, bioenergy, and agricultural products. Environmental policies and programs are formed at all levels—global, continental, national, state, regional, and local. These actions are examples of multilevel governance, where multilevel refers to the interdependence of efforts at several levels of the environment (e.g., ecosystems) and governance to the partnerships and networks among public, private, and nongovernmental organizations involved in the planning and execution of these policies and programs (Bache & Flinders, 2005). For evaluations, analysis at appropriate scales is challenging because it involves assessing projects that (1) are funded by multiple parties, (2) contain different activities (or policies) addressing the same set of actors, and (3) take place simultaneously in attempting to protect, conserve, or enhance the stock of natural resources. Because results of activities across and within projects are not mutually exclusive, attribution at the project level is problematic. The problem becomes more significant owing to inconsistencies in aligning ecological scale to political jurisdiction. Depending on the unit of analysis, scaling causes additional predicaments in discerning exogenous drivers (e.g., climatic patterns) from those endogenous in the projects, programs, and policies subject to evaluation.

The issue of scaling is taken up in Chapter 3 by Hans Bruyninckx, from Catholic University in Belgium. He reviews the evaluation of efforts at eco-regional governance and points to future options for assessing the impact attributed to political jurisdictions that do not align in an ecologically meaningful way. Elizabeth T. Kennedy, Hari Balasubramanian, and William E. M. Crosse give a complementary perspective of this issue in Chapter 4 from Conservation International (CI). Using a case study of their experiences at CI, they examine how information relevant for stakeholders at multiple levels can be produced through "nested scales" organized ecologically using global criteria.

Data Quality and Credibility. Many of the quantitative and qualitative methods commonly used in evaluating development in wildlife and environmental media are severely compromised. The rush to get "data" through approaches such as rapid assessment potentially leads to quantitative and qualitative methods that are both unreliable and of low validity. The adopted methods frequently reflect the bias of the investigator's personal experiences and intellectual predisposition. This creates an urgent need for transparency using common definitions of terms as well as standardized, transparent efforts of data collection and analysis. The methods used to collect and analyze data might be reliable, but when people keep measuring slightly different concepts they cannot be compared.

The first perspective on data credibility is in Chapter 5, by Marc Hockings, Sue Stolton, Nigel Dudley, and Robyn James from Queensland University in Australia. They examine the combined use of quantitative and qualitative data in evaluations, particularly in relation to issues concerning (1) subject matter, (2) scale and timeframe, (3) available resources and data, and (4) risks. The second perspective on data is Chapter 6, by Andrew S. Pullin and Teri M. Knight from the University of Bangor (United Kingdom). They discuss elements of data credibility in applying systematic review methodology to assess the efficacy of conservation interventions on ecological outcomes.

Research Designs. Issues related to casual attribution have long been debated in social sciences and have once again become an important topic in evaluation (e.g., Donaldson & Christie, 2005). Although the issue conceptually is no different in evaluation in the environmental arena from that in other fields, there are specific features that make using counterfactuals in practice daunting. Environmental problems have common characteristics, but they are also unique; no socioecological system is identical to another. To construct any kind of counterfactual (quantitative, or qualitative), only some characteristics of a problem can be taken into account. Difficulties are increased because more often than not the same agent is the subject of multiple interventions. Any simplification using a limited counterfactual is likely to be challenged in a field where the framing of the problems and the relevant context varies greatly with the background and interests of the actors.

Paul J. Ferraro, from Georgia State University, deals with attribution through research designs in Chapter 7. He argues that much of what is called environmental impact evaluation is simply monitoring, and that using counterfactual thinking is crucial for assessing the effectiveness of policies and programs. He examines the barriers to and possibilities for using experimental and quasi-experimental approaches for developing the counterfactual. Richard Margoluis, Caroline Stem, Nick Salafsky, and Marcia Brown provide the complementary view from Foundations of Success (a prominent nonprofit in the conservation community). They explore the range of design options, in addition to those requiring counterfactuals, available for evaluating impact of conservation actions. They assess when certain evaluation designs should be used and identify a plethora of factors that should be taken into account in selecting and implementing a given research design using a quantitative or qualitative approach in dealing with attribution.

This volume concludes with two summarizing chapters. Chapter 9 is by Hallie Preskill, a former president of the American Evaluation Association. She uses her wealth of knowledge of the evaluation field to assess the relevance of the environmental policy and program-specific methodological discussions for evaluators working in other areas. The issue ends with Chapter 10, by the two co-editors, where we offer our own view about four pressing issues that should guide future evaluation efforts in the environmental arena.

References

Bache, I., & Flinders, M. (Eds.). (2005). Multi-level governance. Oxford: Oxford University Press.

Donaldson, S. I., & Christie, C. A. (2005). The 2004 Claremont Debate: Lipsey vs. Scriven—Determining causality in program evaluation and applied research: Should experimental evidence be the gold standard? Journal of Multidisciplinary Evaluation, 3, 60–77.

Hardin, G. (1968). The tragedy of the commons: The population problem has no technical solution; it requires a fundamental extension in morality. Science, 162(3859), 1243–1248.

Hoffmann-Riem, H., & Wynne, B. (2002, March 14). In risk assessment, one has to admit ignorance: Explaining there are things we can't know could improve public confidence in science. Nature, 416, 123.

Kakoyannis, C. (2004). Learning to address complexity in natural resource management. Ph.D. dissertation, Oregon State University.

Mickwitz, P. (2003). A framework for evaluating environmental policy instruments: Context and key concepts. Evaluation, 9(4), 415–436.

Ostrom, E. (1990). Governing the commons: The evolution of institutions for collective action (political economy of institutions and decisions). Cambridge, UK: Cambridge University Press.

Poister, T. H. (2003). *Measuring performance in public and nonprofit organizations*. San Francisco: Jossey-Bass.

Rittel, H., & Webber, M. (1973). Dilemmas in a general theory of planning. *Policy Sciences, 4*(2), 155–169.

Senge, P. (1990). *The fifth discipline: The art and practice of the learning organization*. New York: Doubleday/Currency.

Weiss, C. (1995). The four "I's" of school reform: How interests, ideology, information, and institution affect teachers and principals. *Harvard Educational Review, 4*(65), 571–592.

Wildavsky, A. (1979). *Speaking truth to power: The art and craft of policy analysis*. Boston: Little, Brown.

Wynne, B. (1992). Uncertainty and environmental learning: Reconceiving science and policy in the preventive paradigm. *Global Environmental Change, 2*(2), 111–127.

Matthew Birnbaum
Per Mickwitz
Editors

MATTHEW BIRNBAUM *is an evaluation officer at the National Fish and Wildlife Foundation. Affiliated also with American University, he has been associated with the evaluation field for close to two decades, dealing with a plethora of issues, among them conservation, poverty, alternative modes of transportation, and rural economic development.*

PER MICKWITZ *works as a senior researcher at the Research Programme for Environmental Policy at the Finnish Environment Institute. He is also an adjunct professor of environmental policy at the University of Tampere.*

Hildén, M. (2009). Time horizons in evaluating environmental policies. In M. Birnbaum &
P. Mickwitz (Eds.), *Environmental program and policy evaluation: Addressing methodological
challenges. New Directions for Evaluation, 122,* 9–18.

1

Time Horizons in Evaluating Environmental Policies

Mikael Hildén

Abstract

*Environmental policies have to deal with nonlinear changes, discontinuities, and
thresholds that may unfold with the passing of time. A recursive and adaptive
approach to policy evaluation can deal with these challenges. Key characteristics of adaptive evaluations are their recursive nature, systematic exploration of
multiple intervention theories, and ability to probe into new issues in close interaction with the policy development itself.* © Wiley Periodicals, Inc.

Evaluations are undertaken at specific points in the policy cycle, which
involves preparation, negotiation, implementation, and revision of
policies over time. The relationship of the evaluation to the stage
of the policy cycle affects but does not fix the time horizon of the evaluation. The time horizon in any specific evaluation has to be specified, and the

Note: This study was supported by the Thresholds project of the EU, contract no.
003933.

NEW DIRECTIONS FOR EVALUATION, no. 122, Summer 2009 © Wiley Periodicals, Inc., and the American Evaluation
Association. Published online in Wiley InterScience (www.interscience.wiley.com) • DOI: 10.1002/ev.291

choice is clearly important. It has methodological implications, and it can affect the conclusions of the evaluation drastically.

Standard textbooks on evaluation recognize time series and the temporal sequence of events (Scriven, 1991; Vedung, 1997; Rossi, Freeman, & Lipsey, 1999) but do not pay very much attention to the time horizon as such. This chapter specifically explores the challenges associated with time horizons, an approach I call an adaptive evaluation process. I have borrowed this concept from computer programming (Ennals, 2003) and educational evaluation (Aspden & Helm, 2004), where it means that the evaluation also includes probing; not everything is evaluated at once. The design of the evaluation is such that it retains sufficient flexibility to also refocus on issues that arise in the course of the study even if its original design did not consider them.

A starting point is that the past, present, and future are present in all evaluations but with differing roles and weights. Time perspectives are particularly important in the context of environmental policies because they typically evolve slowly in a series of incremental steps, and any specific policy intervention is strongly path-dependent. This raises a need to look back in ex ante evaluation and to look forward in ex post evaluation.

An adaptive approach means the evaluations are linked to the policy process and they are repeated during the policy cycle; the evaluations become recursive, with possibilities for revisiting findings. Elements for such recursive and adaptive processes already exist. For example, the European Union carries out ex ante evaluations of all significant policy initiatives, and monitoring and ex post evaluations of directives are explicitly required in new legislation.

In adaptive evaluation, the task of successive evaluations is not only to explore the initially identified objectives and side effects but also to probe into some new areas that could reveal new or unexpected impacts. Such a task is challenging from the point of view of a formal evaluation requirement because it is by definition difficult to specify in advance. But the ability to adapt the evaluation to an evolving context clearly has advantages. For example, through probing, the evaluation can maintain the interest of stakeholders, avoid getting locked up in auditing formalism, and also identify at an early stage emerging issues and potentially significant feedback mechanisms.

The Role of Time in Environmental Policies

Environmental policies often require costly transformation of existing practices, infrastructure, or technology. Therefore many processes tend to be slow. For example, it took the international community 11 years to come from UNEP's call to discuss the problem of ozone depletion to the signing of the Montreal Protocol, and still nine more years before the United States actually eliminated production and import of ozone-depleting substances. The ozone layer will not recover until 2060–2075 (U.S. EPA, 2007).

Even more distant futures become relevant in the case of climate policies, or as an extreme case evaluations of nuclear waste policies, which need to consider thousands of years.

An evaluation of environmental policies at any stage of the policy cycle cannot afford to neglect history or the future (see Table 1.1). But the choice of a specific time horizon can nevertheless be contentious. The choice must be based on an understanding of the dynamics of the processes that the policy is intended, or likely, to affect. Some issues can be dealt with using standard approaches borrowed from econometrics. Other aspects require more sophisticated examination of the intervention or program theories in order to correctly identify how the time horizon can affect the outcomes and impact of a policy or policy intervention.

One of the difficulties in specifying a time horizon lies in the nonlinearity or discontinuity of the effects of environmental policies. A further complication involves unknown thresholds or tipping points at which the systems that policies seek to influence may develop relatively suddenly in new directions (Lyytimäki & Hildén, 2007). In combination with relatively long time perspectives, evaluations can therefore seldom produce "the truth." This speaks for adaptive approaches that make it possible to revisit the policy and the evaluations to achieve a deeper understanding of effects and merits, instead of simple checking of deliverables such as creation of a permit system or institutionalization of limit values for harmful substances.

Table 1.1. Time Perspective Versus Type of Evaluation

	Evaluation Relative to the Policy Cycle		
Time Horizon	Ex Ante	Midterm	Ex Post
Past	Recognizing events that will affect the policy but are not part of it; foreseeing and solving in advance the impact problem	Tracking the development of the policy	Examining the origin and history of the policy, its outputs, and its outcomes (impacts)
Present	Correctly identifying the context of the policy	Specifying outcomes and results; dealing with the impact problem	Finding credible solutions to the impact problem; formulating recommendations
Future	Foreseeing the materialization of outcomes and their impacts	Identifying emerging outcomes, results, and impacts; noting the weak signals	Identifying and estimating impacts likely to emerge in order to arrive at fair conclusions on the merits of the policy

Analytical Treatment of Time Horizons

It is common to claim that "short-termism," as reflected in the quarter economy or in the alleged inability of politicians to see beyond their election period, is the root of many evils (see, for example, Third World Network, 1997). There is no doubt that a myopic approach to environmental issues is likely to create problems. At the very least, it fails to solve them.

Differences in length of the time horizon perceived by various stakeholders also frequently cause confusion and fierce debate, as the long-standing battles concerning appropriate discount rate have shown (Arrow, 1999). Despite this, one can argue that length of time horizon is not as such a major problem for evaluations. Although the choice of the time horizon often affects the conclusions and also constrains the analysis, temporal perspectives can be treated analytically and explicitly reported. To deal with time frames one can, for example, vary the time horizon or make sensitivity analyses to explore the consequences of the choice of discount rate.

Approaches that explore the consequences of time horizons are important in evaluation of environmental policies, in particular when one deals with issues that by their very nature have long time horizons. Climate change, boreal forestry management (where a single tree generation may be more than 100 years), and restoration of lakes or coastal waters clearly belong to the kind of policy issues where the choice of discount rate can critically affect the conclusions of an ex ante evaluation. It can also affect ex post evaluations to the extent that the future impact of the policy needs to be addressed. Technically the choice of discount rate is a manageable problem in the sense that it is straightforward to explore the consequences of choices. There is an extensive body of research and also practical guidance to fall back on (HM Treasury, 2003; Cowen, 2008), although each case needs to revisit the basic assumptions in the particular context of the policy.

The analytical treatment of time is likely to raise questions about the nature of future changes. But an adaptive evaluation should combine an examination of discount rates with analysis of feedback mechanisms, uncertainties, and nonlinear change.

Nonlinear Changes, Feedback, and Uncertainties

A greater challenge than the pure length of the time horizon is that uncertainties and outright ignorance increase with an extension of the time line (Hoffman-Riem and Wynne, 2002). The problem is particularly significant in forward extensions of the time line, but extending backward to history also aggravates many uncertainties and opens up room for conflicting interpretations of policies.

An expansion of the historical record may worsen the impact problem (i.e., the difficulty in attributing change or part of it to the intervention; Vedung, 1997). Solving the controversies that arise requires that the evaluator approach her material with the tools and mind-set of a critical historian. Triangulation of data and methods has proven to be useful in demonstrating that anticipation of future policies was in many cases more important than the actual current policy (Hildén et al., 2002; Mickwitz, Hyvättinen, & Kivimaa, 2008). The role of a policy as an indication to actors of the development of future policies should thus also be considered in an evaluation.

With a forward expansion of the time horizon, the likelihood of nonlinear change increases and fundamental assumptions of the whole evaluation exercise can be challenged. The evaluation exercise moves into the realm of "post normal science" (Funtowicz and Ravetz, 1993), which has to deal with a high degree of uncertainty, combined with high stakes in the decisions.

Environmental policies have moved into the postnormal era with policy initiatives for acidifying substances, biodiversity, and above all climate change. A recent international survey directed to experts in coastal and marine management and research showed that experts consider ecological thresholds (i.e., major nonlinear change in the ecosystems) to be likely. At the same time, the experts feel that present policies and management are largely incapable of dealing with thresholds in order to avoid the trespassing of unwanted ones (Lyytimäki, Hildén, Aberra, & Lindholm, 2008).

There are a number of ways to deal with emerging uncertainties and nonlinear changes (Sluijs et al., 2004), and many of the approaches can be applied in adaptive evaluations. For example, actor analysis and critical review of assumptions can be applied as such. A particularly useful approach is to analyze alternative intervention theories (a generic term encompassing program theories but also the underlying logic of, for example, policies and laws) to identify critical assumptions and their temporal dimension. In an adaptive evaluation framework, several intervention theories should be kept and successive evaluations would aim at elucidating which theory appears to correspond to the development as it unfolds.

The detection of feedback loops is essential in evaluation of environmental policy. Causal loop modeling (Sterman, 2000) is one useful tool; it explicitly recognizes that the time horizon is not something that simply extends into the future. Time is also recursive, and a perceptive evaluation of a policy should explore repetitious temporal cycles.

An evaluation of the problems of fisheries regulation using total allowable catch illustrates the recursive nature of policies affecting the environment and the relevance of parallel intervention theories. The basic intervention theory simply says that one can maintain fishing at a sustainable level by constraining the allowable catch. An alternative theory includes a broader context, taking into account the possibility and likelihood of nonreporting of catches, discarding, etc. Successive evaluations can explore each of the complicating features in order to determine which are significant for implementation of the policy. This kind of comparative adaptive approach can also be useful in evaluating innovative new regulatory practices or combined with other approaches such as the limiting factor analysis.

Another type of temporal uncertainty that evaluations of environmental policies have to recognize are those related to nonlinear changes and discontinuities caused by the emergence and diffusion of social and technological innovations. These innovations can be the result of policies or specific policy interventions and should be addressed in evaluation. The emergence of environmentally benign innovations is implicitly or explicitly one of the key objectives of environmental policies (Kivimaa, 2008). Yet this aspect has only recently received greater interest as an evaluation task (Brunnermeier and Cohen, 2003; Frondel, Horbach, & Rennings, 2004; Foster, Hildén, & Adler, 2006).

The analysis of potential innovations requires careful analysis of the intervention theories. There are many approaches that can help the evaluator do this systematically. Examples are causal loop modeling (Sterman, 2002), the PROTEE method (Hommels, Peters, & Bijker, 2007) and strategic niche management (or SNM; Geels & Schot, 2007). Their perspectives differ, and the choice of approach should therefore depend on what is being evaluated. Causal loop modeling is good for highlighting feedback links. The SNM approach can identify protective niches where the likelihood of radical innovation is likely to increase. The PROTEE method systematizes risks and opposition to the innovation.

So far, many of the approaches to evaluating the emergence of innovations have been applied in ex post analyses, but there is an obvious need to explore innovation in ex ante evaluations of environmental policies. Climate change and other global environmental issues require that environmental policies contribute significantly to nothing short of radical innovation. This requires recognition of the time horizon of innovations, and evaluations should explore how policies can affect the likelihood of new innovations. The task cannot be handled properly unless one uses an adaptive evaluation approach that explores numerous scenarios.

Scenarios and Their Time Horizons in Adaptive Evaluation

Scenarios have a dual role in evaluation of environmental policies. Scenarios that are used as a basis for policy development can themselves be evaluated, but scenarios can also be used as tools in conducting adaptive evaluation.

The time horizon of the scenarios used for policy development is conceptually easy to evaluate, but the task is important. For example, in the first Finnish national climate and energy strategy of 2001, the time horizon was defined as generally limited to 2010 with some general considerations of the development until 2020 (Council of State, Finland, 2001). The ex ante evaluation clearly indicated this to be too myopic, and no real differences could be discerned between the scenarios that had been used as a basis for the policy (Hildén, Attila, Hiltunen, Karvosenoja, & Syri, 2001). The criticism of the time frame was also repeated by the Parliament in its conclusions on the strategy (Environment Committee, 2001). The strategy prepared in 2008 included scenarios extending to 2050 (http://www.tem.fi/?l=en&s=2658 [April 23, 2008]).

The second role of scenarios in evaluation is more demanding but necessary in ex ante evaluations and also in ex post evaluations, if there are significant outcomes and impacts that have not yet materialized at the time of the evaluation. For example, a fierce debate in biodiversity conservation deals with the issue of extinction debt (Tilman, May, Lehman, & Nowak, 1994; see also Gullison & Hardner in this issue). The only way to address the risk of future extinctions is through scenarios, but it is also necessary to evaluate such scenarios because some may be based on overly pessimistic or optimistic intervention theories.

Estimation of future changes in species abundance requires detailed examination of habitat transformation and specific habitat characteristics. Such tools are becoming available but need to be backed up by expert judgment and also a good historical record. Auvinen et al. (2007) combined expert judgments of the development of populations of threatened species with modeling of forest stands, in particular the amount of dead wood, and examination of remote sensing data for pilot areas in order to come to conclusions on the successes and challenges of the countrywide biodiversity policy. Gullison and Hardner (see elsewhere in this issue) argue likewise for validating the views of practitioners with those of experts.

Even though scenarios are developed to explore possible outcomes and impacts rather than to predict specific ones, evaluators are faced with the dilemma that they need to say something on the likelihood of the various scenarios. A common way around the problem is to provide conditional evaluations, which state the key factors that are likely to affect the development. Another possibility is to use tools from strategy development, such as SWOT analysis (internal strengths and weaknesses plus external opportunities and threats) or best case, worst case dichotomies. These approaches are useful because they allow actors to identify their own views and put them in context. By formulating the context under which a particular outcome or impact can appear, the evaluator can contribute to a social learning process that can be followed up in successive evaluations.

Conclusions: Adaptive Evaluation Can Address Key Issues Related to Time Horizons

In an ex post evaluation the time horizon can be extended both backward and forward. Backward extension may help in revealing path dependencies and also in addressing to what degree impact is induced by the intervention and how much it is caused by other factors, thus reducing the risk of falsely attributing change to a program that has simply coincided with a change that was already initiated earlier. This is very much in line with evaluation

NEW DIRECTIONS FOR EVALUATION • DOI: 10.1002/ev

approaches such as realistic evaluation (Pawson & Tilley, 1997) or theory-driven evaluations (Chen, 1990). Forward extension of the time horizon may be crucial for correct inferences concerning the effectiveness of a policy or program. Changes initiated by a program may initially appear insignificant, but detection of a cumulative nonlinear change fed by a feedback loop may radically alter the view. An enhanced ability to detect feedback loops is one of the greatest strengths of an adaptive evaluation approach.

In ex ante evaluation, the forward extension of the time horizon is particularly demanding. A single projection far into the future is usually not meaningful, but even a suite of projections may give a false sense of controllability unless the possibility of thresholds of radical change is recognized. This requires merging future-looking innovation research with evaluations.

One of the crucial consequences of extending the time horizon is that evaluations have to recognize the possibility that self-organizing and emerging features of social systems (Hernes & Bakken, 2003) become significant. In the case of environmental policy evaluations, this means first of all that the evaluations are linked to the policy process and that they are repeated during the policy cycle; the evaluations become recursive, with possibilities for revisiting findings.

To make the adaptive evaluation feasible, some items will also have to be dropped in each evaluation round. The criteria for dropping an item can be that no new information has accumulated since the last round, or that the previous evaluation already came to a definitive conclusion concerning its merits. For example, the first evaluation of the Finnish national climate strategy offered a general overview of the issues. The second evaluation, which was made to support a revision of the strategy, included heavy emphasis on issues of adaptation to climate change. The third evaluation dropped this item because it had become a topic of its own and focused instead on a life cycle assessment of the policy measures and topics surrounding health impacts as well as those involving bioenergy.

By adopting a recursive and adaptive approach, one can deal in environmental policy evaluations with the challenges embedded in the time horizons. They can also then contribute genuinely to a social learning process and avoid the fate of becoming mere ritual in the bureaucratic machinery.

References

Arrow, K. J. (1999). Discounting, morality and gaming. In P. R. Portney & J. P. Weyant (Eds.), *Discounting and intergenerational equity*. Washington, DC: Resources for the Future.

Aspden, L., & Helm, P. (2004). *Researching networked learning: Critically reviewing an adaptive evaluation*. Presented at the Networked Learning Conference 2004. Retrieved June 5, 2008, from http://www.networkedlearningconference.org.uk/past/nlc2004/proceedings/individual_papers/aspden_helm.htm

Auvinen, A.-P., Hildén, M., Toivonen, H., Primmer, E., Niemelä, J., Aapala, et al. (2007). Evaluation of the Finnish National Biodiversity Action Plan 1997–2005. *Monographs of the Boreal Environment Research, 29*, p. 54.

Brunnermeier, S. B., & Cohen, M. A. (2003). Determinants of environmental innovation in U.S. manufacturing industries. *Journal of Environmental Economics and Management, 45*(2), 278–293.

Chen, H.-T. (1990). *Theory driven evaluations.* Newbury Park, CA: Sage.

Council of State, Finland. (2001). *National Climate Strategy: A report to the Parliament.* VNS 1/2001 vp, Helsinki (in Finnish).

Cowen, T. (2008). Social discount rate. In S. N. Durlauf & L. E. Blume (Eds.), *New Palgrave Dictionary of Economics* (2nd ed.). London: Palgrave Macmillan; *New Palgrave Dictionary of Economics Online.* Palgrave Macmillan. http://www.dictionaryofeconomics.com/article?id=pde2008_S000464>doi:10.1057/9780230226203.1554

Ennals, R. (2003). Optimistic evaluation: An adaptive evaluation strategy for non-strict programs. In *ICFP, '03: Proceedings of the Eighth ACM SIGPLAN International Conference on Functional Programming.* Retrieved June 5, 2008, from http://research.microsoft.com/Users/simonpj/Papers/optimistic/icfp2003.pdf

Environment Committee, Finnish Parliament. (2001). *The Committee's Report on the National Climate Strategy.* YmVM 6/2001 vp—VNS 1/2001 vp, Helsinki (in Finnish).

Foster, J., Hildén, M., & Adler, N. (2006). Can regulations induce environmental innovations? An analysis of the role regulations in the pulp and paper industry. In J. Hage & M. Meeus (Eds.), *Innovation, science, and institutional change: A handbook of research* (pp.122–140). Oxford: Oxford University Press.

Frondel, M., Horbach, J., & Rennings, K. (2008). *What triggers environmental management and innovation? Empirical evidence for Germany* (RWI: Discussion Papers No. 15). Retrieved May 30, 2008, from http://repec.rwi-essen.de/files/DP_04_015.pdf

Funtowicz, S. O., & Ravetz, J. R. (1993). Science for the post-normal age. *Futures, 25*(7), 739–755.

Geels, F.W., & Schot, J. W. (2007). Typology of sociotechnical transition pathways. *Research Policy, 36*(3), 399–417.

Hernes, T., & Bakken, T. (Eds.). (2003). *Autopoietic organization theory: Drawing on Niklas Luhmann's social system perspective.* Copenhagen Business School Press.

Hildén, M., Attila, M., Hiltunen, M., Karvosenoja, N., & Syri, S. (2001). *Environmental assessment of the national climate strategy.* Helsinki, Finland: Finnish Environment Institute, 482 (in Finnish)

Hildén, M., Lepola, J., Mickwitz, P., Mulders, A., Palosaari, M., Similä, J., et al. (2002). Evaluation of environmental policy instruments: A case study of the Finnish pulp and paper and chemical industries. *Monographs of the Boreal Environment Research, 21*.

HM Treasury (2003). *The green book appraisal and evaluation in central government.* London: TSO. Retrieved March 30, 2008, from http://www.hm-treasury.gov.uk/d/green_book_complete.pdf

Hoffman-Riem, H., & Wynne, B. (2002). In risk assessment, one has to admit ignorance. *Nature, 416*, 123.

Hommels, A., Peters, P., & Bijker, W. E. (2007). Techno therapy or nurtured niches? Technology studies and the evaluation of radical innovations. *Research Policy, 36*(7), 1088–1099.

Kivimaa, P. (2008). *The innovation effects of environmental policies: Linking policies, companies and innovations in the Nordic pulp and paper industry.* Acta Universitatis Oeconomicae Helsingiensis A329, Helsinki School of Economics. Retrieved April 4, 2009, from http://hsepubl.lib.hse.fi/pdf/diss/a329.pdf

Lyytimäki, J., & Hildén, M. (2007). Thresholds of sustainability: Policy challenges of regime shifts in coastal areas? *Sustainability: Science, Practice, and Policy, 3*(2), 1–9. http://ejournal.nbii.org/archives/vol3iss2/communityessay.lyytimaki.html

Lyytimäki, J., Hildén, M., Aberra, Z., & Lindholm, M. (2008). The significance of ecological thresholds in coastal areas: Results of an international web survey. *Reports of
the Finnish Environment Institute, 21*. Retrieved September 10, 2008, from http://www.
ymparisto.fi/default.asp?contentid=294589&lan=en&clan=en

Mickwitz, P., Hyvättinen, H., & Kivimaa, P. (2008). The role of policy instruments in
the innovation and diffusion of environmentally friendlier technologies: Popular
claims versus case study experiences. *Journal of Cleaner Production, 16*(1S1), 162–170.

Pawson, R., & Tilley, N. (1997). *Realistic evaluation*. London: Sage.

Rossi, P. H., Freeman, H. E., & Lipsey, M. W. (1999). *Evaluation: a systematic approach*
(6th ed.). London: Sage.

Scriven, M. (1991). *Evaluation thesaurus* (4th ed.). Newbury Park, CA: Sage.

Sluijs, J. P., van der, Janssen, P.H.M., Petersen, A. C., Kloprogge, P., Risbey, J. S.,
Tuinstra, W., & Ravetz, J. R. (2004). *Tool catalogue for uncertainty assessment* (2004.
RIVM/MNP Guidance for Uncertainty Assessment and Communication. Report nr:
NWS-E-2004–37). Retrieved May 20, 2008, from http://www.nusap.net/downloads/
toolcatalogue.pdf

Sterman, J. D. (2002). *Business dynamics: Systems thinking and modelling for a complex
world*. New York: McGraw Hill.

Third World Network. (1997). TNCs and globalisation: Prime sources of worsening ecological crisis. *Third World Resurgence, 81/82*. Retrieved September 10, 2008 from
http://www.twnside.org.sg/title/pri-cn.htm

Tilman, D., May, R. M., Lehman, C. L., & Nowak, M. A. (1994). Habitat destruction and
the extinction debt. *Nature, 371*, 65–66.

U.S. EPA. (2007). *Achievements in stratospheric ozone protection* (U.S. EPA Publication
EPA-430-R-07–001). Retrieved May 22, 2008, from http://www.epa.gov/ozone/2007
stratozoneprogressreport.html

Vedung, E. (1997). *Public policy and program evaluation*. New Brunswick, NJ: Transaction.

MIKAEL HILDÉN *is a professor at the Finnish Environment Institute's Research
Department in Helsinki.*

Gullison, R., & Hardner, J. (2009). Using limiting factors analysis to overcome the problem of long time horizons. In M. Birnbaum & P. Mickwitz (Eds.), *Environmental program
and policy evaluation: Addressing methodological challenges. New Directions for Evaluation,*
122, 19–29.

2

Using Limiting Factors Analysis to Overcome the Problem of Long Time Horizons

Raymond Gullison, Jared Hardner

Abstract

*In recent years, donors to biodiversity conservation projects have sought greater
accountability, using professional evaluators to help assess the degree to which
grantees are achieving conservation objectives. One of the most formidable challenges evaluators face is the time required both for ecological systems to respond
to management interventions and over which grantees must maintain their biodiversity conservation gains. The authors present a simple methodology, called
limiting factors analysis, which was developed during the course of evaluating
several large portfolios of conservation projects. The method is a practical basis
for rapidly assessing whether current conditions are likely to prevent grantees
from achieving their long-term objectives. Use of the methodology is illustrated
with examples from recent evaluations of the Andes Amazon Initiative and the
Columbia Basin Water Transactions Program.* © Wiley Periodicals, Inc.

B iodiversity conservation projects attempt to halt or reverse the loss of the
world's species and ecosystems through diverse activities, including
restoring natural habitats, creating incentives for less destructive natural
resource use, reintroducing species into areas where they have disappeared,

and managing protected areas. Biodiversity conservation receives substantial support from philanthropic and government funders in the United States and abroad. For example, James, Gaston, and Balmford (2001) estimated that approximately $6 billion was spent annually managing the global protected areas network in the mid-1990s. Over the past decade, both donors and conservation practitioners have shown increased interest in monitoring the effectiveness of these investments (see Hockings, 2003; and CMP, 2008, for some examples).

There are various methodological challenges to evaluation of biodiversity projects and programs. In this chapter we draw on our recent experience in evaluating large biodiversity conservation programs to discuss a pragmatic approach we have used to overcome one such obstacle: the long time horizons that evaluators must grapple with when considering the merits of the biodiversity programs they are evaluating.

An obvious problem that the sometimes slow pace of ecological change can cause for evaluators is that the impacts of anthropogenic activities—both good and bad—can take a very long time to manifest. It may take decades or even hundreds of years to fully restore certain types of ecosystems or to recover a species. For example, the official recovery plan for the red cockaded woodpecker (RCW) describes a detailed series of measures that experts feel will be sufficient to prevent the species' extinction in the Southeastern United States (USFWS, 2003). Even with the substantial effort implied by the plan, the recovery team does not expect to remove the RCW from the endangered species list until 2075—nearly 100 years after formation of the original recovery plan. The problem that these long time horizons present for evaluators is clear. The current condition of a species or ecosystem may offer few clues as to the long-term success of the management actions that are the focus of the evaluation.

A related problem is that the one-to-three-year duration typical of funding for biodiversity conservation activities is usually much shorter than the time horizons relevant to biodiversity conservation projects. Evaluations conducted with the primary purpose of demonstrating accountability to donors must somehow deal with the disparity in time horizons between the funding they have awarded and the time required for ecological systems to respond.

A final problem is that even if ecological change does occur over a short time period, many of these gains need to be maintained in perpetuity if they are to have value. The long-term likelihood of success of a conservation program must therefore be a paramount consideration in the evaluation.

Of course, long time horizons are not a problem unique to evaluation of biodiversity conservation projects. However, well-designed, statistically rigorous trials available in other fields (e.g., medical trials; see Everitt and Pickles, 2004) are challenging to implement for biodiversity conservation projects. Among the reasons are (1) insufficient resources available to set up and monitor trials and (2) difficulty in selecting appropriate control sites and replication because of the unique nature of species and ecosystems.

NEW DIRECTIONS FOR EVALUATION • DOI: 10.1002/ev

Furthermore, because of the long time horizons required to see ecological change, it will depend on the conservation practitioners themselves, rather than the evaluators coming in at a later date, to set up long-term trials and conduct ecological monitoring. However, our experience is that few conservation practitioners are creating the conditions that would allow for a meaningful evaluation of impact at a later date. The urgency of implementing conservation actions and a general shortage of resources mean that allocation of resources to collecting baseline information, performing ecological monitoring, and conducting internal evaluation and formal adaptive management is typically meager, and we do not see strong indications that this situation is likely to change, at least in the near future.

Yet these obstacles must not be used as an excuse to avoid evaluating biodiversity conservation projects (Sutherland, Pullin, Dolman, & Knight, 2004; Ferraro and Pattanayak, 2006). Resources for conservation are scarce and must be allocated to greatest effect. Evaluation can help make the most of the limited resources available for biodiversity conservation.

Limiting Factors Analysis

The remainder of this chapter describes an approach to evaluating biodiversity conservation projects that helps address the problem of long time horizons. The basis of the approach is to work with the donor and grantees to develop a common understanding of the key factors that must be assessed, and if necessary (and possible) managed, for the biodiversity conservation project or program to be viable over the long run. This is a simple and qualitative approach to forecasting, with the goal of identifying currently unmanaged factors that are likely to prevent the grantee from achieving its objectives. We call this approach a "limiting factors analysis," borrowing the term *limiting factor* from the agricultural and ecological literature (van der Ploeg, Bohm, & Kirkham, 1999), where its use refers to the factor or factors that have the greatest influence in limiting the growth or abundance of an organism. In a similar spirit, we use the term to refer to those factors that present the greatest threat to a biodiversity conservation project.

Many factors may limit the ability of a conservation project to achieve its long-term conservation objectives, among them financial, policy, scientific, and social factors. These limiting factors may extend well beyond the boundaries of the project itself, requiring grantees and evaluators to consider the broadest possible context in which the conservation project is taking place. Thus evaluators must attempt to get the big picture and assess whether everything necessary is being done to reduce both short- and long-term risks to the conservation target, even if it is beyond the scope of what many would consider to be the grantee's normal activities.

We have found a consistent list of limiting factors relevant to a broad range of project types and ecological systems:

New Directions for Evaluation • DOI: 10.1002/ev

- *Scientific understanding* that is inadequate to formulate appropriate management actions to sustain the conservation target
- *Public policy* that does not support conservation of the target
- *Legislation* that does not offer sufficient legal protection to the conservation target
- *Institutional capacity* that is inadequate to perform conservation activities
- *Economic pressures* that cause destruction of the conservation target
- *Enforcement* of laws and regulations that is inadequate to implement the legislation on the ground to protect the conservation target
- *Stakeholder support* that is inadequate to conserve the target
- *Short-term funding* that is insufficient to establish an adequate level of conservation management, including capital expenditures on equipment and infrastructure
- *Long-term funding* that is inadequate to support the recurrent costs of conservation management activities

Although some categories may not be fully independent (e.g., legislation obviously influences enforcement, and availability of finance underpins institutional capacity), each category brings unique information for consideration. This list has been for us a useful starting point for evaluating a spectrum of biodiversity conservation programs in numerous locations.

We follow a three-step process to customize the list of limiting factors for each evaluation.

Step one: identify limiting factors. First, we ask grantees, stakeholders, and experts to review the core list of limiting factors and suggest the addition of other limiting factors, as appropriate to their project. This step yields a list of limiting factors as specific as possible to the program being evaluated. However, if a program has many project types, then the limiting factors must be defined very broadly (see the next section, "Case Studies").

Step two: score limiting factors. Next, we work with grantees and others to rank the status of each limiting factor when the grantee began its activities (a retrospective baseline), and then again at the time of project completion (or point of evaluation, if grants are ongoing). We use a small number of coarse ordinal scoring categories ranging from "presenting a complete impasse to conservation" to "does not limit conservation in any way."

Step three: understand the management response. We then ask grantees and others to identify all of the entities (conservation groups, government agencies, and so on) that are working at overcoming the various limiting factors, their source of funding, how they are going about it, and their likelihood of success.

It is useful at this stage to consider whether limiting factors are internal or external to the project. Internal factors result from the activities of grantees (for example, failure to carry out the necessary science to support project activities, insufficient engagement with project stakeholders to secure their support for a project), while external factors derive from outside of the boundaries or limits of the project (for example, economic forces causing habitat and species loss). Grantees must also consider the degree of control or influence they have on the limiting factor. The time horizon is an important consideration here; as an example, over a short time period of one or several years grantees may have little influence over a particular piece of counterproductive legislation. However, over a longer time period grantees may in fact be able to work with others to influence legislators and effect change.

A particularly important class of limiting factors is external factors that are a serious or complete barrier to the long-term conservation of the target, and over which the grantee has no influence. If these factors exist, and if grantees cannot change their own activities to reduce the impact of these factors, donors and grantees may question whether the project is worth continuing.

Information gained through site visits and interviews with independent stakeholders of the projects allows us to verify the information gained in steps 1 through 3. Application of the limiting factor analysis permits a number of useful observations:

- At the project level, it helps us understand how strategic grantees have been in prioritizing their activities, and the progress they have made on the limiting factors they are working on.
- At the site level, it helps us understand whether all the important limiting factors are being addressed, or whether important unmanaged limiting factors or weak links of the chain remain that threaten conservation at the site.
- At the program level, it helps us understand whether the program has a balance of project types that are an appropriate response to the most important factors limiting the conservation of the target, or whether some rebalancing would be beneficial.

Of course, situations are dynamic, and even if a project, site, or program receives high marks for resolving limiting factors this does not guarantee that it will achieve its long-term biodiversity conservation objectives. The exercise is, however, very useful in identifying situations where the converse is true, namely, identifying situations where conservation gains are unlikely to materialize or be sustained over time because of the failure of a grantee to address factors that are limiting the conservation of the target.

Case Studies

We illustrate the utility of the limiting factors analysis with several examples. The first is our evaluation of the Gordon and Betty Moore Foundation's Andes Amazon Initiative, or AAI (Hardner et al., 2006). AAI seeks to contribute to the preservation of the biodiversity and hydrologic function of the

Amazon Basin. Failure to maintain a critical threshold area of forest cover may put the entire basin's hydrology and biodiversity at risk (Shukla, Nobre, & Sellers, 1990). At the time of the evaluation, AAI had determined that an additional 140 million hectares of protected areas were needed, and that effective management of the basin's entire protected area complex would need to be put in place, presumably in perpetuity.

Only time will tell whether the objectives of creating and effectively managing enough protected areas to conserve the basin's biodiversity and hydrologic cycle are achieved. At this early stage in the program, a major goal of the evaluation was simply to determine whether there were unaddressed limiting factors that would raise doubts as to whether AAI and its grantees could achieve their goals. We developed a list of factors relevant to AAI projects that were capable of limiting or even preventing long-term conservation of individual protected areas (these are the same as the core list presented above). We then surveyed grantees, interviewed project stakeholders, and visited project sites to score each limiting factor before and after AAI's investment at all of the sites where its grantees worked (Figure 2.1). This identified those factors grantees were successfully managing (for example, enforcement of conservation laws and building institutional capacity) and those that grantees were not (such as securing adequate short- and long-term financing). It also identified the factors most likely to prevent achievement of long-term objectives, the most important of which was the inability of grantees to secure adequate financing for long-term management

Figure 2.1. Progress on Limiting Factors Made by Grantees in the Andes Amazon Initiative (AAI)

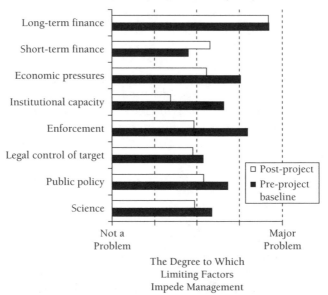

of the sites. These findings led to specific oversight and monitoring suggestions for the program, including development of a long-term financing strategy to support protected areas in the region.

Our 2006 evaluation of the Columbia Basin Water Transactions Program (CBWTP) is the second example of use of the limiting factors methodology (Hardner & Gullison, 2007). The CBWTP is a partnership between Bonneville Power Administration and the National Fish and Wildlife Foundation (NFWF). The goal of CBWTP is to support nongovernmental organizations and state agencies in acquiring water rights for the benefit of salmon and other fish species in the Columbia Basin, located in the northwestern United States. CBWTP's grantees are experimenting with various types of innovative water transactions and seeking to integrate their efforts with those of other groups working on other aspects of habitat restoration that together will lead to fully restored fish habitat.

A key focus of the evaluation was to examine the potential of CBWTP to scale up and address the water flow needs of all priority rivers and streams in the Columbia Basin. The youth of the program made addressing this question challenging. At the time of the evaluation the program was only in its fourth year, which was too early to demonstrate ability to implement water transactions on a large geographic scale, or demonstrate that it could maintain biologically significant water flows over a long period of time. The limiting factor analysis was very helpful in anticipating CBWTP's ability to grow to the scale it desired. Working together with grantees and program staff, we developed a list of limiting factors relevant to the CBWTP program. Because grantees worked in the same basin and conducted similar activities, we were able to develop a list of limiting factors that was much more detailed than in the case of the AAI, though the broad categories of limiting factors were very similar. The grantees then rated each limiting factor for subbasins where they worked.

The results (partially shown in Figure 2.2) clearly identify those factors that grantees have effectively mastered (such as the ability of grantees to monitor water flow and other aspects of compliance to the transactions), and those factors that are creating a serious impediment or impasse to work for the majority of grantees (poor coordination of donor support, high transaction costs) and hence are presenting barriers to scaling up the number of water transactions in the Columbia Basin and beyond. The evaluation concluded that none of the factors most limiting grantee efforts pose insurmountable problems, but they do demand increased attention from both grantees and program staff alike if CBWTP is to reach the scale it desires.

Discussion

The limiting factor analysis is not a stand-alone approach. It is meant to complement other evaluation approaches, such as assessing the scientific basis of project activities, the degree to which project activities are

Figure 2.2. Some Factors Limiting the Ability of the Columbia Basin Water Transactions Program (CBWTP) Grantees to Expand Their Work

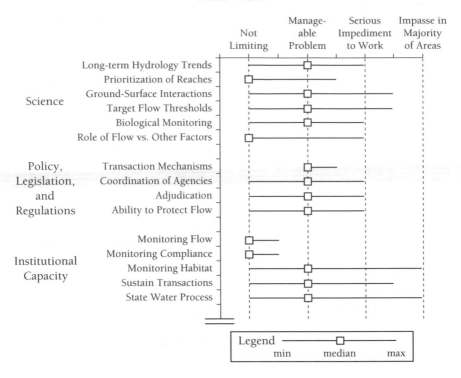

adequately resourced and implemented, and the degree to which projects address conservation priorities. As we have attempted to demonstrate in this chapter, the role of limiting factors analysis is to help us anticipate or forecast the long-term fate of biodiversity conservation projects. It does this by assessing the extent to which practitioners have identified and are managing (if possible) the full range of social, economic, ecological, and other factors that might jeopardize the project and threaten its long-term viability. As such, it is one way of at least partially addressing the problem that the long time horizons characteristic of biodiversity conservation projects present to evaluators.

Our approach has evolved independently of, but has much in common with, other evaluation approaches that attempt to assess the degree to which conservation practitioners are adequately diagnosing and managing the factors influencing the outcome of their projects. Salafsky and Margoluis (1999) and Hockings (2000) usefully review other threat-based approaches to evaluation of biodiversity conservation projects. The Threat Reduction

Assessment (TRA) presented by Salafsky and Margoluis (1999) is perhaps one of the best known. Both TRA and the limiting factor analysis ask grantees to systematically assess the immediate importance of specific threats to the sites where they work and judge the effectiveness of their response to them. However, the TRA is a more formalized process, meant as an in-depth management planning tool for specific sites, in addition to acting as the basis for assessing the effectiveness of management of these threats. Our limiting factor analysis should be considered more as a process, designed for evaluators, grantees, and other stakeholders to rapidly gain an understanding of the context in which grantees are working (the limiting factor list can often be developed in an afternoon with grantees and other stakeholders), often across broad portfolios of hundreds of project types. Another difference between the two approaches is that the TRA normalizes threats and threat reduction at every site with a threat reduction index. This is a very useful approach for grantees for every site to identify priority actions. In contrast, our approach does not normalize scores, which is useful for donors who may wish to compare conservation needs across sites (rather than within a site) when deciding how to prioritize their investments. A final difference is that TRA focuses on current direct threats to biodiversity (such as logging and hunting that are actually taking place). In contrast, the limiting factor analysis casts its net broader and farther into the future by also including other factors such as long-term financing and the policy and legal framework that will ultimately determine the ability of a biodiversity conservation project or program to manage any and all threats that appear down the road. This is a particularly important difference because as evaluators we need to anticipate the long-term fate of projects, not just consider how they are responding to current challenges.

The limiting factors analysis also has features in common with empowerment evaluation (Fetterman, Kaftarian, & Wandersman, 1996). Both approaches engage program participants to develop a framework for evaluating past program performance. However, the emphases of the two approaches differ. In combination with other methodologies, we use limiting factor analysis as a methodology to contribute to an accurate understanding of a program's true impact to date, and we build in considerable third-party consultation to both develop the limiting framework and verify the status of limiting factors. In contrast, the goal of empowerment evaluation is to engage mainly program participants, particularly those whose voices are not necessarily heard or valued as much as those in power, in a forward-looking strategic planning and adaptive management process.

We cannot see any reason in principle for the limiting factor analysis methodology not to be useful in other environmental fields where similar approaches do not already exist. One obvious application is helping to assess the long-term sustainability of natural resource management, such as forests or fisheries. In fact, the certification standards that have evolved to assess the sustainability of some natural resources (e.g., the Forest Stewardship Council standards for forest management) include a comprehensive list of social, economic, and environmental limiting factors that must be met for a particular managed forest to be certified. A similar extension can be made to other areas of practice in the public and nonprofit sectors where donors and grantees operate on a short-term time frame directed toward long-term results.

We find that the limiting factor methodology evolves and improves with every new application. One area where we seek further improvement is in developing ways to reduce the subjectivity of grantees and stakeholders in scoring the extent to which particular factors are impeding conservation at their sites. This may best be accomplished by coming up with increasingly detailed and objective criteria for every possible score that can be assigned to the limiting factors. It is particularly important that grantees at different sites interpret the rankings consistently if the results are to be compared across sites, and that diverse voices be included in the process to ensure that all relevant factors are identified and considered. When the evaluation budget and scope allows, we reduce subjectivity by verifying grantee ratings with site visits and interviews with project stakeholders. In the future, we will also seek validation of the approach itself by comparing the fate of biodiversity conservation projects having unmanaged important limiting factors with the fate of those projects that were characterized in earlier evaluations as effectively managing their limiting factors.

In conclusion, we look forward to the day when grantees are able to integrate more sophisticated evaluation and monitoring into their own projects, including ecological monitoring of their conservation targets, and when grantees have track records commensurate with the time horizons required to detect changes in natural systems. Until that time, however, we have to rely on pragmatic approaches such as the one described here to evaluate grantee accomplishments and understand the long-term likelihood of success.

References

Conservation Measures Partnership (CMP). (2008). About CMP. Conservation Measures Partnership Web site. Retrieved May 29, 2008, from http://www.conservation measures.org/CMP/About.cfm

Everitt, B., & Pickles, A. (2004). *Statistical aspects of the design and analysis of clinical trials*. London: Imperial College Press.

Ferraro, P. J., & Pattanayak, S. K. (2006). Money for nothing? A call for empirical evaluation of biodiversity conservation investments. *PLoS Biology, 4*(4), e105 doi:10.1371/journal.pbio.0040105.

Fetterman, D. M., Kaftarian, S. J., & Wandersman, A. (1996). *Empowerment evaluation: Knowledge and tools for self-assessment and accountability*. London: Sage.

Hardner, J., & Gullison, R. E. (2007). Independent external evaluation of the Columbia Basin Water Transactions Program. Unpublished report presented to the Columbia Basin Water Transactions Program. www.nwcouncil.org/fw/program/2008amend/ cbwtp.pdf

Hardner, J., Gullison, R. E., Flynn, S., Qayum, S., Kometter, R., Akella, A., et al. (2006). Independent external evaluation of the Andes-Amazon Initiative of the Gordon and Betty Moore Foundations (2001–2005). Unpublished report presented to the Gordon and Betty Moore Foundation, San Francisco.

Hockings, M. (2000). *Evaluating protected area management: A review of systems for assessing management effectiveness of protected areas*. University of Queensland, School of Natural and Rural Systems Management.

Hockings, M. (2003). Systems for assessing the effectiveness of management in protected areas. *BioScience, 53*(9), 823–832.

James, A., Gaston, K. J., & Balmford, A. (2001). Can we afford to conserve biodiversity? *BioScience, 51*(1), 43–52.

Salafsky, N., & Margoluis, R. (1999). Threat reduction assessment: A practical and cost-effective approach to evaluating conservation and development projects. *Conservation Biology,13*, 830–841.

Shukla, J., Nobre, C., & Sellers, P. (1990). Amazon deforestation and climate change. *Science, 247*(4948), 1322–1325.

Sutherland, W. J., Pullin, A. S., Dolman, P. M., & Knight, T. M. (2004). The need for evidence-based conservation. *Trends in Ecology and Evolution, 19*, 305–308.

U.S. Fish and Wildlife Service (USFWS). (2003). *Recovery plan for the red-cockaded wood-pecker (Picoides borealis): Second revision*. Atlanta, GA: U.S. Fish and Wildlife Service, Southeast Region.

van der Ploeg, R. R., Bohm, W., & Kirkham, M. B. (1999). On the origin of the theory of mineral nutrition of plants and the law of the minimum. *Soil Science Society of America Journal, 63*, 1055–1062.

RAYMOND GULLISON and JARED HARDNER are partners in the private consulting firm Hardner & Gullison Associates, based in New Hampshire. Gullison is also an honorary research associate at the Centre of Biodiversity Research at the University of British Columbia in Vancouver.

Bruyninckx, H. (2009). Environmental evaluation practices and the issue of scale. In
M. Birnbaum & P. Mickwitz (Eds.), *Environmental program and policy evaluation: Addressing
methodological challenges. New Directions for Evaluation, 122*, 31–39.

3

Environmental Evaluation Practices and the Issue of Scale

Hans Bruyninckx

Abstract

*Social scientists, natural scientists, and evaluators have not properly defined the con-
cept of scale for environmental problems. Environmental scale generally differs from
social scale, which confounds the challenge of evaluating policies and governance
arrangements in addressing environmental issues. Instead, social scales are generally based on traditional jurisdictional boundaries, and this complicates effective decision making. Conversely, evaluators must be able to assess innovative governance
arrangements as well as the outcomes of environmental problems because the two
are interconnected. This is particularly true in looking at cross-scale, social-
ecological interactions. This has profound implications for policy evaluation; evaluators have to develop frameworks for connecting across various scales and levels
in overcoming mismatches. Natural scientists probably need to be humbler in their
ambitions, and evaluators will have to engage in interdisciplinary teams that blend
the expertise of the social sciences with that from the natural sciences to assess outcomes to social and environmental scales.* © Wiley Periodicals, Inc.

E nvironmental policy making is increasingly based on an ecosystemic,
an eco-regional, or more broadly an ecological logic. This creates the
need to adopt practices of policy formation and policy evaluation to

NEW DIRECTIONS FOR EVALUATION, no. 122, Summer 2009 © Wiley Periodicals, Inc., and the American Evaluation
Association. Published online in Wiley InterScience (www.interscience.wiley.com) • DOI: 10.1002/ev.293

this new logic (Cowling & Pressey, 2003; Noss, 2003; Groves, 2003; Leroy & Bruyninckx, 2006). Examples can be found in water management, where river basin approaches, even on a very small scale, are increasingly the norm (Folke, Hahn, Olsson, & Norberg, 2005); in transboundary nature protection projects supported by the European Union (EU directive 79/409/EEC); or policies on migratory species, which often link distance locations on the basis of an ecological logic. These policies do not follow the classic territorial boundaries of policy making. To the contrary, they involve "natural" geographic delineations, multiple (overlapping) policy institutions, and often unfamiliar funding constructions. In addition, they increasingly are based on collaboration between state actors at different levels, civil society actors and market actors. They are, in other words, what are nowadays known as governance arrangements (Spaargaren, Mol, & Bruyninckx, 2006).

These new governance arrangements are creating challenges for existing institutions and practices, because they are functioning at different "scales." The need for serious evaluations of these arrangements is strong for several reasons. Policy arrangements that are supposedly more properly adapted to the ecological-scale level are based on the promise of leading to better performance. It is only normal that they are assessed with regard to those promises (Spaargaren, Mol, & Buttel, 2006). Also, given the emphasis on environmental rationality for the scale of the social intervention, more attention is going to environmental outcomes, whereas environmental (policy) evaluations are usually preoccupied with the institutional aspects (Gysen, Bruyninckx, & Bachus, 2006).

In the first part of this chapter, the meaning of the scale concept is explained. This first step is necessary because the concept is generally underdefined and underspecified. The second part makes the link with environmental policy making. Starting from the assumption that scale is indeed an important concept, it is vital to think about the possible consequences for policy makers and stakeholders. Third, I pay attention to the impact for environmental evaluators. The chapter ends with a number of ideas about the further use of scale as a concept, including possible consequences.

The Concept of Scale in Environmental Policy Making

If scale is not adding anything to our understanding of environmental problems, the societal responses that we have formulated to deal with them, or our capacity to evaluate these two matters, then the concept has little use (Goertz, 2005). To the contrary, adding a redundant concept might make debate more difficult (Sartori, 1970). By using scale as a key to effective policy responses and allocation of resources, we are taking a clear position: scale *is* adding something to our understanding. It has an impact on defining issues, collecting data at the appropriate level, identifying resources and stakeholders that function at this particular scale, and formulating policy.

Although numerous subfields define scale, I limit the debate to what is crucial for environmental policy evaluation: environmental scales and scales of social organization.

A *social definition* of scale refers to levels of social organization relevant to understand the driving forces and societal responses to environmental issues. We use the concepts of driving force and societal response based on the DPSIR model (Driving forces–Pressures–State of the environment–Impact–Responses) in use by the EU (EEA, 2001). Through a logical chain, it links social phenomena to ecological issues. It thus refers to systems of production and consumption and to types of social intervention, including policy making, to remediate or solve environmental problems. An *ecological definition* of scale is based on the environmental unit of analysis. Determining the relevant unit on the ecological scale is crucial, according to ecologists and environmental scientists, in determining the appropriate matching unit of analysis of understanding or intervention on the social scale.

There are different *levels* along each scale. For example, on the ecological scale there is the global eco-systemic level and also the plant level. Similarly, on the scale of social organization we can, for instance, distinguish the level of globalized social practices and also the household level. We can thus scale up or scale down levels on a scale.

Problems of Scale and Environmental Policy Making

Institutional Fit Problem: Scale Mismatch Between Ecological and Social Scales. The incompatibility of scale refers to the fact that the scale of the environmental problem does not coincide with the social scale (i.e., level of the policy intervention). When this is the case, some authors refer to the necessity of scaling the problem up or down (Young, 2002; Gupta, 2005). One can ask about the added value of using scale to discuss political or administrative levels in this case. More appropriate concepts seem to be available (e.g., centralization and decentralization, devolution, local, subnational, national, or international policy levels). However, incompatibility of scales refers not only to specific levels (being points along the scale) but to the disjointed nature of alignment between spatial and social scales as well. At a more fundamental level, our knowledge systems, policy models, environmental models, and social organization have been dominated by an approach that separates these scales (Homer-Dixon, 2002).

Scale mismatch needs to be taken seriously. In nearly all international policy documents on environmental problems, the issue of scale plays a central role. The choice of policy level—the one at which participation is to be organized, or the level of understanding of driving forces—is an important matter. Making the wrong choices can have serious consequences for the effectiveness and efficiency of social interventions (Young et al., 2006). Most of the literature references regarding scale are about the level of governance, or in other words, the social scale. The link with the ecological scale is much less explicit. Much more attention will have to go there in the future if we want to overcome the problem of institutional fit.

Mismatch Between Policy Scale and the Scale of Knowledge Creation. Cash and Moser (2000, p. 235) describe mismatch as "discordance between the scale of scientific analysis and assessment and the scale for which scientific information is needed to usefully inform management and policy makers." Although elaborate measuring and monitoring schemes are present in most OECD countries, and modeling capacity for complex environmental issues and database management techniques and reporting initiatives exist, there remains a problem of mismatch between the available information and the information needed to create a better match between ecological and social scales.

Creating more adapted knowledge seems rather easy, yet it is more complex than it appears. The knowledge and information systems that feed into policy decisions are mostly embedded in institutionalized practices of monitoring, measuring, analyzing, and reporting. Changing these systems involves technical changes and costs. More fundamental is that scaling knowledge production up or down requires serious epistemological rethinking and constructing new explanatory models (see also Kennedy et al. in this issue). Linking ecological scale to social scale assumptions requires bridging natural and social science knowledge and searching for essential epistemological connections. Given the possible difficulties and the costs, as well as the potential societal benefits, public support for this type of exercise would seem appropriate.

Cross-Scale Interactions. Interactions between environmental scale levels are one of the core dynamics studied by ecologists. Interactions between scales and actors operating at different social scale levels are the essence of the concept of multilevel and multiactor governance. Horizontal and vertical integration of social practices in the field of the environment and sustainable development are now standard expectations (Bruyninckx, 2006). These issues of cross-scale interactions make policy arrangements even more complex.

New governance arrangements of driving forces and responses, operating on the basis of multiactor and multilevel dynamics, seem to be our best answer. Innovative, more flexible instruments and the so-called networked organization of societal responses are in my opinion mostly still in the experimental phase. Much needs to be done in this domain, and according to important sociologists our capacity to create fundamental synergies between our social scale responses and the ecological scale will be necessary if we want to have a chance in light of the enormous environmental challenges (Castells, 2000; Urry, 2003).

Scale and Environmental Policy Evaluation

Expectations of higher efficiency and effectiveness are formulated because interventions are (supposedly) more adapted to appropriate scale levels. The difficult task of demonstrating whether this is the case is the task of the evaluator. The challenge for evaluators is to develop innovative methodologies for assessing effectiveness and efficiency.

In addition, evaluators *can* play a role in tackling some of the more essential problems outlined here. By entering into the core debate about scales, including fit, mismatch, and interaction problems, evaluators can become an important partner in the necessary debate regarding these issues. This assumes that evaluators acquire knowledge about these problems, realize how they have an impact on their profession, and are able to formulate goals regarding their own contribution in the debate.

To acquire more insights in this matter, it seems necessary to take a closer look at how evaluators are confronted with the essential problems of scale and policy making as outlined in the previous section.

Institutional Fit and the Mismatch of Scale. In the case of mismatch between the environmental scale and the social scale, evaluators can play a pivotal role in creating a better institutional fit. High-quality evaluation both on the side of the environment and of the social and policy processes can potentially provide essential information about the lack of institutional fit and the necessary steps to be taken to create a better match. The problem of mismatch of scale prompts us to ask questions about the necessity to make more explicit linkages between ecological approaches of evaluation and policy approaches. Too often these follow separate trajectories, cater to different audiences, and hardly know of one another's existence. However, there is generally little holding back in ambitions: policy evaluations often use elements of ecological scale without much background knowledge, and ecological approaches to environmental evaluation include institutional claims and suggestions for institutional or policy change. This is generally based on common sense, experience, or underestimation of the institutional complexity and societal dimensions of environmental problems. The same is true when it comes to explicit evaluation of economic driving forces, or possible economic uses (e.g., market instruments), in policy making. Conceptualizing economic mechanisms as an essential component of the driving forces or the responses is a difficult task requiring specialist knowledge.

This leads to a call for more serious efforts to do interdisciplinary evaluations. I realize that this call is controversial, for several reasons. It has been around for some time and has not produced much in terms of results. It also goes against the basic knowledge tradition of which we are a part. Yet environmental issues are almost by definition complex and multidimensional and require interdisciplinary approaches. To support those policy efforts, evaluators will have to follow. Although it may be bold, I dare to say that evaluators can do more than follow. By bridging disciplinary barriers in their work, they can demonstrate leadership in examining how multidisciplinary approaches can uncover weaknesses in policy making and in fit.

Creating Knowledge at the Right Scale Level. Although the issue of knowledge creation at the relevant scale level might seem less of a responsibility or an issue for the evaluator, there are a number of issues related to evaluation with regard to knowledge creation and knowledge adaptation (Leroy and Bruyninckx, 2006).

Data gathering, which is a key element for evaluation of environmental policy, becomes more complex when innovative policy arrangements across typical political and administrative scales are set up. In many cases, the systems for data gathering are in line with the scale of the dominant social scale levels: countries, provinces or states, or municipalities. A serious shortage is the gathering of data that link the driving forces explicitly to the environment. Another problem, especially when needing data for transboundary policy interventions, is the *comparability of data.* Evaluators working for different counties, states, or provinces have experience in this matter. Even when it is not their explicit task to look at data comparability, they often have better knowledge of these differences in data gathering than the actors themselves. Yet probably the most fundamental problem is that the *relevance of data* often depends on mostly implicit definitions of both ecological and social scale that have served as the context for the policy. When the context changes (e.g., from a provincial scale to a watershed), the chance that the existing data, or the data gathering systems, are relevant is small. In thinking about solutions for this problem, I believe that two elements seem crucial. First, much closer attention should be paid to the fundamental questions regarding the type of knowledge we need. The challenge is to furnish knowledge that is relevant for the scale of the problem and the scale of the social intervention. This presupposes better understanding of both social and environmental dynamics and the interplay between both. Environmental evaluators could permit insights into the processes and dynamics of current systems in order to improve them.

These three essential problems will require increased attention in the future. Evaluators are well placed to detect possible problems because they need specific information to do their evaluations in a sound methodological way. By reporting and explaining existing problems, they can be triggers for change. Moreover, the collaboration between ecological and social scale evaluators seems fundamental to get a comprehensive understanding of the necessary knowledge.

Cross-Scale Interactions. Cross-scale interactions are probably the most difficult for evaluators. The difficulty of doing decent evaluations at one scale and one level is already a challenge. When asked to evaluate the dynamics that exist across scales, in function of better societal responses, one can mention several problems. Linking scales means the evaluator needs an understanding of those scales and the interactions between them. This adds to the knowledge requirements and the capacities of evaluators. Only in rare instances will all of this be present in a single individual. This means that interdisciplinary teamwork has to become the norm. It probably means that evaluators will have to set up flexible networks for generating knowledge and applying methods that can impart the necessary combination of professional expertise and skill.

An additional but second-order problem for the evaluator is the fact that those responsible for policy interventions along different scales are usually not very much organized to absorb recommendations aimed at cross-scale interactions. Our model of policy organization, based on compartmentalized policy domains, separate policy levels, and bureaucratic organizations, seems contradictory to tackling the effects of cross-level interactions.

Other Issues for Environmental Policy Evaluators. There are consequences of more scale-conscious evaluation practices for the demand side of evaluations. Agencies, bureaucracies, foundations, etc., have to be aware of the issues of scale that have been discussed. Again, evaluators have a role to play, or even a responsibility. "Educating" the demand side (including the client) might be an important component of precontract negotiations. Shaping new agendas for environmental evaluation is a difficult task, requiring knowledge about the substantive environmental issues, about the policy processes or intervention strategies, and about evaluation. Most often, the client does not combine all of this. The evaluator can help to understand new demands, shape new agendas, make arguments for funding, etc. This is a slow and iterative process, requiring active interaction—for example, through forums that link academic communities to commercial evaluators and government actors, all excellent arenas to have this sort of discussion. The Environmental Evaluators Network, in essence a coordinated effort by the EPA and the NFWF to bring together representatives from those three communities to exchange publications that cater to those three audiences, is another possibility. Flexible boundaries in career paths also help. Because in-house evaluators are increasingly part of policy-making institutions, chances are they will end up in the private sector or pursue advanced graduate work according to their experience. In the other direction, experienced evaluators can be hired by the government, as is increasingly the case for those with advanced academic training. Important also is the potential role of the NGO sector; a vital part of the methodological innovation in evaluation stems from their demands and their attention for more scale-adapted analyses.

The *institutionalization* of evaluation at other than the standard or regular policy level is a challenge of its own yet is, in my opinion, the most important decision to be made regarding evaluation. Institutionalization means that environmental evaluation will be part of the normal, standard policy-making process, and this happens at the relevant levels of the ecological and social scale. This is far from evident, even at some of the dominant scales of environmental policy making, i.e., the national level and the state or provincial level (the highest subnational level). Only when policy evaluation becomes fully institutionalized will it be seen as an integral part of policy making. At this time, it is mostly conceptualized after policies are in the phase of implementation and perceived as an additional add-on. It rarely belongs to the core of policy making and policy learning.

NEW DIRECTIONS FOR EVALUATION • DOI: 10.1002/ev

Conclusions

I have demonstrated that questions of scale are relevant for environmental policy making. The next question, then, is whether this has an impact on the work of environmental evaluators. In my opinion, it does. It complicates the task of evaluators as new and fundamental problems surface when taking scale more carefully into account; problems of fit, mismatch, and interaction all apply. This is a rather uneasy conclusion; environmental evaluation as we know it today is already struggling with conceptual issues, epistemological foundations, sound methodologies, complexity, and interdisciplinarity. Adding the issue of scale might be a bit overwhelming.

One has to realize two fundamental realities, however. First, the issue of scale has always been implicitly present, and making it explicit will in the end make things easier by forcing us to come up with better approaches. Second, paying closer attention to issues of scale can and will make the work of evaluators and their results even more relevant than today. However, this prompts evaluators to become more conscious, more professional, more interdisciplinary, and more aware of the complexity of things. I have tried to demonstrate that the reality of evaluation work is such that three main actors will have to be included in order to overcome these challenges: (1) evaluators as the professionals in the field; (2) natural and social scientists with particular expertise in studying the environment and ecosystems because they possess the fundamental knowledge used by evaluators to shape their methodologies; and (3) users of evaluations because they know in the end which types of evaluation really further the processes, actions, programs, or other intervention they are managing and implementing.

In conclusion, I offer four concrete elements for evaluators to start thinking about scale in their own work. First, ask yourself at what level along the social or environmental scale you are doing your evaluation, and make it explicit. Second, pay attention foremost to the problem of fit. Giving policy advice for a scale level that does not fit is a waste of time and resources because it does not contribute to better policies. Third, think about what you can contribute, through your expertise as an evaluator, to the fundamental debate on the knowledge we need to make more "scale-conscious" policies, and the type of cross-scale interactions. Finally, confront yourself with your own limits: Are you able to grasp all of this by yourself, or do you need to see yourself as a member of a team of "scale-knowledgeable" evaluators?

References

Bruyninckx, H. (2006). Sustainable development as a contested policy concept. In D. Stevis, M. M. Betsill, & K. Hochstettler (Eds.), *International environmental politics.* Palgrave Academic Press.

Cash, D. W., & Moser, S. C. (2000). Linking global and local scales: Designing dynamic assessment and management processes. *Global Environmental Change, 10*(2), 109–120.

Castells, M. (2000). *The rise of the network society* (2nd ed.). Vol. I of *The information age: Economy, society and culture.* Oxford: Blackwell.

Cowling, R. M., & Pressey, R. L. (2003). Introduction to systematic conservation planning in the Cape Floristic Region. *Biological Conservation, 11*, 1–13.

European Environment Agency (EEA). (2001). *Reporting on environmental measures: Are we being effective?* (Environmental Issue Report No. 25). Copenhagen: European Environment Agency.

Folke, C. Hahn, T., Olsson, P., & Norberg, J. (2005). Adaptive governance of social-ecological systems. *Annual Review of Environment and Resources, 30*, 441–473.

Goertz, G. (2005). *Social science concepts: A user's guide.* Princeton, NJ: Princeton University Press.

Groves, C. R. (2003). *Drafting a conservation blueprint: A practitioner's guide to regional planning for biodiversity.* Washington, DC: Island Press.

Gupta, J. (2005). *Global change: Analysing scale and scaling in environmental governance.* Unpublished manuscript, Free University Amsterdam.

Gysen, J., Bruyninckx, H., & Bachus, K. (2006). Evaluating effectiveness of environmental policies: The modus narrandi. *Evaluation, 12*(1), 95–118.

Homer-Dixon, T. (2002). *The ingenuity gap: Facing the economic, environmental, and other challenges of an increasingly complex and unpredictable world.* New York: Random House.

Leroy, P., & Bruyninckx, H. (2006). Beleidsevalautie en Milieubeleid. Hoofdstuk 1 in Crabbé, Joos Gysen, Pieter Leroy. *Vademecum Milieubeleidsevalautie.* Vanden Broele: Brugge.

Noss, R. (2003). A checklist for wildlands network designs. *Conservation Biology, 17*(5), 1270–1275.

Sartori, G. (1970). Concept misinformation in comparative politics. *American Political Science Review, 6*(4), 1033–1053.

Spaargaren, G. A., Mol, P. J., & Bruyninckx, H. (2006). Introduction: Governing environmental flows in global modernity. In G. A. Spaargaren, P. J. Mol, & F. H. Buttel (Eds.), *Governing environmental flows: Global challenges to social theory.* Boston: MIT Press.

Spaargaren, G. A., Mol, P. J., & Buttel, F. H. (Eds.). (2006). *Governing environmental flows: Global challenges to social theory.* Boston: MIT Press.

Urry, J. (2003). *Global complexity.* Cambridge, MA: Polity Press.

Young, O. R. (2002). *The institutional dimensions of environmental change: Fit, interplay, and scale.* Cambridge, MA: MIT Press.

Young, O. R., Berkhout, F., Gallopin, G. C., Janssen, M. A., Ostrom, E., & van der Leeuw, S. (2006). The globalization of socio-ecological systems: An agenda for scientific research. *Global Environmental Change, 16*, 304–316.

HANS BRUYNINCKX is a professor of environmental politics at the Leuven University in Belgium.

Kennedy, E. T., Balasubramanian, H., & Crosse, W.E.M. (2009). Issues of scale and monitoring status and trends in biodiversity. In M. Birnbaum & P. Mickwitz (Eds.), *Environmental program and policy evaluation: Addressing methodological challenges. New Directions for Evaluation, 122,* 41–51.

4

Issues of Scale and Monitoring Status and Trends in Biodiversity

Elizabeth T. Kennedy, Hari Balasubramanian,
William E. M. Crosse

Abstract

Designing a framework that can generate data to meet multiple audience objectives must consider interactions across levels and multiple scales of interest. One solution is to define targets using global criteria such that units are discrete. This aids identification of the types of data to collect in order to enable aggregation and reporting across relevant scales. By striving to standardize measurable targets and data requirements, we improve our ability to format monitoring information and tailor indicators for different reporting and decision-making purposes. We outline the application of a nested approach presently used by Conservation International and describe some of its advantages and limitations. © Wiley Periodicals, Inc.

Ultimately, monitoring and evaluation serve management and decision makers as a guide to demonstrate progress and adapt strategies and actions to improve efficiency in achieving objectives over time. The natural resource management and biodiversity conservation community is increasingly recognizing the importance of scale in implementation

and evaluation of policy and actions (Boyd et al., 2008; Adger, Brown, & Tompkins, 2006; Reid, Berkes, Wilbanks, & Capistrano, 2006; Folke et al., 2002; Lovell, Mandondo, & Moriarty, 2002; Poiani, Richter, Anderson, & Richter, 2000). Accordingly, several nations, agencies, and organizations are using planning and decision frameworks that attempt to integrate multiple scales. Consistent with Cash et al. (2006), we use the term *scale* to refer to the dimension used to measure or study a phenomenon (e.g., spatial, juris-dictional) and *level* as the unit of analysis situated along the continuum of a particular scale. For example, the biodiversity scale can be viewed as a hierarchy of levels, including genes, species, populations, communities, landscapes, and biosphere, with each level (unit of analysis) exhibiting char-acteristic composition, structure, and function (Noss, 1990). We summa-rize additional examples of scales of interest and corresponding levels from Cash et al. (2006) in Figure 4.1.

The subsequent complexity associated with addressing and under-standing the challenges that arise from cross-scale dynamics (Cash et al., 2006; Lovell et al., 2002) requires that the design of monitoring and evalua-tion strategies take scale and cross-scale dynamics into account so that obser-vations and analyses are appropriate and results can inform management decisions. In the conservation community, we face two prominent scale-related challenges. The first is that ecological processes and biodiversity are often not bound by lines on a map or traditional human management frame-works and therefore can be expressed differently across spatial, jurisdictional, and management scales. The second is ensuring that information with rele-vant ecological meaning is available for decision making at multiple levels of

Figure 4.1.   Schematic of Possible Scales and Levels (Circles) of Interest to Be Considered in Design of Monitoring and Evaluation Systems

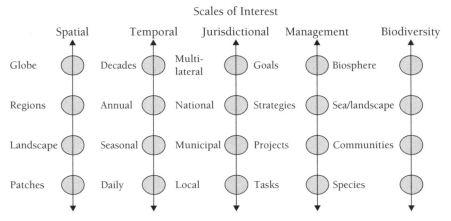

Note: The levels represented are not an exhaustive list.

Source: Modified from Cash et al. (2006).

NEW DIRECTIONS FOR EVALUATION • DOI: 10.1002/ev

jurisdictional and management scales. For a more detailed discussion on these cross-scale issues, see Hans Bruyninckx's article in this issue.

This chapter presents experiences at Conservation International as a case study. We outline two ways to overcome the identified scale-related challenges: (1) setting discrete targets that characterize complex biodiversity components as globally consistent units of analysis reflecting respective levels on the biodiversity scale, and (2) adopting a nested monitoring approach to enable identification of information needs and purpose across jurisdictional and management scales. We discuss the design of this monitoring framework, how it has been implemented, and key relative strengths and weaknesses. We organize the chapter by key issues needed to facilitate efficient multilevel monitoring design, regardless of content domain:

1. What is the consistent theme of the work, and how is it defined?
2. What is the purpose, or what are the questions that need to be answered?
3. Who are the stakeholders that require information, and what information is needed?
4. What are the strategies for meeting information needs?

Identifying and Defining Consistent Theme

The term *target* is used here to narrow the scope of focus for investment, action, and measurement, or the subset of things on which we want to focus. For example, among the entire set of species in the biosphere, we may want to focus only on a particular subset such as birds. Several biodiversity conservation organizations target taxonomic groups or particular systems (e.g., wetlands) in their work. Using the species example, CI focuses conservation action on those species that are globally threatened according to the International Union for Conservation of Nature Red List.

Historically, the conservation community has lacked clear definition of which aspects of the environment were targeted. In the biodiversity conservation realm in particular, there are differing opinions about the purpose for conservation, or even the definition of biodiversity in all its complexities. They range from the degree of interest in individual units of biodiversity (genes, species, communities) to the value that biodiversity offers to humans (watershed management, climate regulation). Although all definitions of biodiversity have merit, some have a less practical application when considering a results-based approach. This has impeded our ability to conclusively and quantitatively demonstrate that conservation actions are (1) the right ones, (2) in the right place, and (3) achieving the conservation results we intend. We view this absence as a major constraint in reporting on the status and trends of biodiversity.

Any definition of a set of systematic biodiversity outcomes will likely not be all encompassing, but it is at least a basis for decision making and measuring conservation progress. Following the sentiment outlined by Noss (1990), we employ a discrete characterization of biodiversity, describing major components at multiple levels of ecological organization. This lays the foundation of a conceptual framework for identifying specific, measurable indicators to monitor change and assess the overall status of biodiversity irrespective of level of investment (local, regional, or national) or type of intervention (protected area, ecotourism, or legislation).

We strive to identify conservation targets that are discrete and measurable entities; are consistent across spatial, jurisdictional, temporal, and management scales as well as ecological systems; and can be replicated over time. These targets are defined at three levels of ecological organization: species (globally threatened species), sites (key biodiversity areas), and sea or landscapes (important conservation corridors and area-demanding species that cannot be conserved at one site).

Targets are defined at levels of ecological organization that (1) are easily discernible; (2) permit direct measurement; (3) are independent of spatial scale; and (4) can be defined in a systematic, repeatable way using globally consistent criteria. Parts of this process have been documented (Langhammer et al., 2007; Conservation International, 2004; and Eken et al., 2004). This approach helps CI define a consistent theme yet still allows inclusion of many elements of biodiversity and other goals conservation projects may have.

Purpose of Monitoring

Using a hierarchical approach to define targets that nests species within sites and sea and landscapes as well as sites within the broader sea or landscape (Figure 4.2) allows monitoring attributes at all levels of ecological organization and at different degrees of resolution according to management questions and objectives. Here is where we pose the critical questions of relevant information needs and purpose for monitoring and evaluation. Monitoring can yield a variety of information that is useful to many parties. However, without clear understanding of the questions monitoring and evaluation systems are trying to address, decisions made using the data, and likely resultant actions taken, monitoring can be misdirected. One of the broadest complaints about implementing monitoring and evaluation plans is that information is not relevant to questions that are posed at the end of an investment cycle. It is crucial to identify information needs at the outset; there is little point in collecting information if it is not known how it will be used. This is true regardless of the level of reporting. We identify two primary categories of questions:

1. Those that address broad patterns and trends irrespective of direct action or investment. The purposes are to identify gaps and prioritization of investment and action as well as demonstrate achievement of defined target status.

NEW DIRECTIONS FOR EVALUATION • DOI: 10.1002/ev

Figure 4.2. Visualization of Nested Nature and Distribution of Discrete Conservation Targets (Globally Threatened Species, Sites of Global Conservation Significance, and Landscapes Required for the Persistence of Globally Threatened Species)

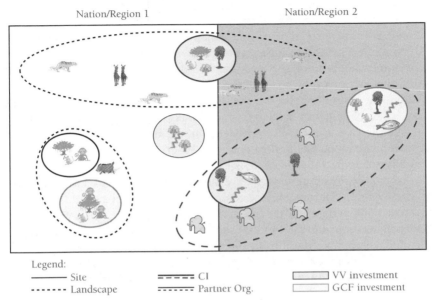

Note: The targets are distributed across spatial scales (sites and landscapes), political boundaries (nation/regions 1 and 2), management entities (Conservation International [CI] and partner organization), and investment portfolios (Verde Ventures [VV] and Global Conservation Fund [GCF]).

2. Those that address process-related trends relative to a direct action or investment. The purposes are to facilitate adaptive management of an intervention or project as well as demonstrate that the project is achieving objectives and ultimately improving the status of the defined target.

Where the primary interest is broad patterns of change (e.g., national reporting on protected area network development; or percentage of globally threatened species for which protection, monitoring, and required research are in place), a globally consistent set of standard indicators facilitate identification of gaps and prioritization of investments. This overarching monitoring framework, called status monitoring by CI, allows us to understand the status of biodiversity and can be reported for a local, regional, national, portfolio, institutional, or global set of targets. The primary utility or purpose of this type of monitoring is to identify gaps and better prioritize investment and action. It also facilitates our ability to demonstrate achievement of defined targets and objectives where investments and actions occur. This framework allows summary of data across multiple interventions and sociocultural, political, and ecological circumstances. It can be used to describe the achievement of high-level goals such as those set by a given investment portfolio, institution, or international consortium (e.g., Convention on Biological Diversity [CBD] 2010 Target).

For issues that are process related (e.g., how does a specific management action affect the conservation target?), we employ measurement that affords a higher resolution of information, which CI calls intervention monitoring. Intervention monitoring measures variables that relate changes in the conservation target (species, site, and sea or landscape) relative to specific threats and a specific action or set of actions. This allows practitioners to begin to test defined assumptions related to management objectives and better apply adaptive management practices for individual projects. As we begin to amass data using a results-based approach, our ability to predict impacts and desired results is substantially enhanced. Practitioners can be more efficient and effective when this learning is captured consistently and transparently. With intervention monitoring we examine changes in the entire assumed chain of events (biodiversity status, threats, and actions within an area of interest). These data can then be used to test assumptions of whether and how actions contribute to biodiversity status changes. Table 4.1 summarizes the chief characteristics of this nested approach to monitoring.

The use of criteria to define conservation targets that standardize complex biodiversity components at a global level constitutes a consistent base from which to use monitoring data across various scales, whether spatial, jurisdictional, or managerial. Through monitoring, information is generated that can be appropriately aggregated, analyzed, and shaped to respond to management objectives, decision making needs, and reporting levels. Principally, we generate information about the individual conservation target (the most fundamental unit) so we can present the results depending on the type of question or management decision being made. We can slice the data for a given project, generate national or regional reports, and report for a specific investment portfolio, institution, or the entire set of conservation targets for the globe (see Figure 4.2) to address the relevant question category or need.

Information Types and Stakeholders

The combination of targets defined using global criteria and specified reporting objectives or decision making needs aids identification of types of data to collect in order to enable aggregation and reporting for respective audiences. Understanding the information needs among end users is essential in creating a system that is viewed as beneficial for most; accordingly, it is crucial to identify stakeholders. Stakeholders include both data users and providers. A universal stakeholder, regardless of level on the reporting scale, is the donor; its requests should always be considered. Typically there are a variety of stakeholders at each level of reporting. These groups are often not

Table 4.1. Reporting Level, Reporting Objectives, Decision Support, Information Types, and Strategies for Information Collection Characteristics of a Nested Monitoring Approach

Characteristic	Status, Outcome Monitoring	Intervention Monitoring
Reporting level	Level at which the decision and action need to be taken (e.g., individual conservation target [species, site, sea or landscape], region, nation, institution, portfolio, globe)	Level at which the project or intervention is implemented
Primary reporting objectives and purpose	(1) Demonstrate status of predefined targets irrespective of investment or conservation action; (2) evaluate progress toward and achievement of targets in predefined commitments (e.g., grant agreements; regional, national, and multilateral agreements such as the Convention on Biodiversity 2010 Target); (3) identify common themes, persistent issue, or major problems faced by projects in a portfolio	Demonstrates effectiveness of a given intervention in achieving stated objectives; facilitates evaluation of a given intervention type (e.g., ecotourism, conservation concession)
Decision support	Identify gaps, prioritize action and investment	Adaptive management of the project or intervention
Information type	Standardized, globally consistent state, pressure, response, and implementation variables for each conservation target level	Unique state, pressure, response, and implementation variables for the assumed results chain to be achieved by project or intervention
Strategies to collect information	Establish networks that link data users and providers, ideally through open access data management platforms	Imbed within grantee agreements or requests for funding so it becomes fundamental to project implementation

uniform and represent heterogeneous aspirations and needs for monitoring information. It is important to recognize this and take time to identify both data users and providers as well as establish a process to facilitate communication with these constituencies.

Through our experience, we have found that involving a variety of stakeholders at the outset of design is crucial to facilitate design, data sharing, and processes that inform planning, learning, and adaptive management. This is especially true of national and regional monitoring efforts because no single organization or government has the financial or human capacity to independently conduct this work; therefore efforts to implement monitoring across these levels are contingent on collaboration among, and participation from, a variety of actors (notably those who see value in data for national and regional reporting and decision-making purposes). This includes (1) NGOs engaged in local, national, and regional level conservation and development planning; (2) private sector firms such as those in oil and gas or tourism industries; (3) governmental bodies required to report against national, regional, and multilateral level obligations; and (4) civil society, which individually and collectively has positive and negative ecological footprints. Equally it is important to include academic and scientific institutions with a focus on research and monitoring, protected area managers, and community groups.

Strategies to Generate Information and Outputs

Although interested parties will likely carry out data collection and analysis, ensuring the sustainability of long-term monitoring programs is also dependent on building confidence among information providers that the data they make available will be managed responsibly, interpreted accurately, and disseminated to key audiences with their best interests in mind. Recognizing these partners also as important data users is one way to address these concerns.

Establishing networks is essential to achieving collaborative, integrated approaches that generate coherent alliances recognizing linkages across levels and scales. Binding stakeholders together instigates a collective focus on what capacity building and funding needs must be addressed to permit sustainable biodiversity data collection, management, analysis, and reporting. Maintaining such a coordinated approach to monitoring requires sustaining linkages between ongoing initiatives, enhancing information sharing, and defining clear roles and responsibilities among key stakeholders. Networks have an ultimate goal of ensuring that biodiversity monitoring is embedded in future conservation strategies and acknowledged as a central means for prioritizing and planning conservation investment.

For monitoring that serves to address the specific question of whether a project is achieving objectives, the best strategy to ensure generation of data is to imbed these practices and requirements into grantee agreements and the standards and practices for any specific intervention type implemented as a conservation strategy. Ideally the utility of outputs from intervention monitoring results in the intervention type or project being able to demonstrate effectiveness in achieving defined objectives and ultimately improvement in the status of the conservation targets. Thus these projects or intervention types enjoy both a competitive edge in accruing additional financial resources and key information useful for ongoing development of strategies to achieve objectives.

NEW DIRECTIONS FOR EVALUATION • DOI: 10.1002/ev

Key Challenges

By using a hierarchical set of biodiversity conservation targets (species, sites, sea and landscapes) and nesting the monitoring approach, we can report at the relevant management decision-making level and allow straightforward translation and aggregation of data on the status of biodiversity. The nested approach permits measurement of all three levels of ecological organization with a dual lens: we generate data on the status of the conservation target and overall patterns of biodiversity using a standardized set of indicators; and, where we have a direct investment, we generate data on the effectiveness of that investment, looking at changes in status of the specific threats to the conservation target, actions taken, and resulting changes in the state of the conservation target. Use of globally consistent conservation targets permits data comparability across targets and reporting units. Further, it ensures compatibility between information generated to look at gaps in investment and achievement of defined target status to evaluate achievement of project objectives to inform adaptive management. This nested monitoring system recognizes the importance of scale in monitoring and evaluating for conservation. Ideally, by establishing a clear ecological basis for monitoring and using a nested approach, effects of actions and stresses will be observed as they are expressed through the multiple levels of ecological organization, allowing certain spatial, jurisdictional, and temporal phenomena to be captured and addressed in a timely fashion.

Use of this nested framework maximizes the generation of data as well as promotes development of more effective measures and expands the scope of measures across geographic areas. It produces a basic set of data on biodiversity that are feasible and affordable to collect and make it globally assessable. We take advantage of otherwise scattered data and make them useful and more readily available, allowing key gaps to be identified and addressed. This is a step in meeting some of the key data gaps outlined by Ferraro and Pattanayak (2006); Mace et al. (2005); Pullin, Knight, Stone, and Charman (2004); Balmford, Green, and Jenkins (2003); and Royal Society (2003). We attempt to meet the need to transparently communicate basic information related to achievement of a discrete set of conservation targets using globally consistent criteria to build public awareness and direct relevant policy decisions.

There are several challenges to establishing and sustaining any monitoring and evaluation approach. Many get mired in articulation of the standardized variables that need to be measured. There are differing viewpoints of what is important and how to measure variables, and discussions often never get beyond examining what to measure. A key learning is to select a few measures for each target level that all stakeholders view as relevant to their decision-making needs. As the framework is implemented, it gains validity, applicability, and ultimately sustainability, permitting additional refinement of the framework in terms of methodological approaches and additional variables. To achieve coherence between the levels of reporting, it is critical to identify what the purpose and key questions are at each level. This permits description of how the data need to be translated across levels where possible and identification of what is unique to that level of reporting or decision making. It is also crucial to establish functioning networks in order to link data uses and data providers so that the linkages between levels are maintained. Our experience to date has taught us that a number of principles help to establish functional networks:

- There is a collective focus or clear need for the network to function (e.g., government declarations to deliver expansion of protected area network, or multilateral agreements such as the Convention on Climate Change)
- No one organization can meet all measurement and reporting needs, so it is important to identify synergies at cross-level and cross-scale interactions
- An accessible data management system is required, as is describing and addressing data interoperability as well as different ways to access and distribute data (Web-based systems with various levels of access as well as hard copy exchanges)
- Networks must address the realities of many players, so there is a need for participatory platforms and appropriate time lines for each actor to articulate and identify methods to address needs and concerns in an ongoing manner

Finally, the ever-present challenges of resource constraints (both capacity and financial) are relevant in implementing this multilevel framework. It is necessary to ensure time and financial resources to build capacity in multiple sectors (government, academic, private, nongovernmental organizations, local project managers) to provide, analyze, and use data for their respective needs.

References

Adger, W. N., Brown, K., & Tompkins, E. L. (2006). The political economy of cross-scale networks in resource co-management. *Ecology and Society, 10*(2), 9. http://www.ecologyandsociety.org/vol10/iss2/art9/

Balmford, A., Green, R. E., & Jenkins, M. (2003). Measuring the changing state of nature. *Trends in Ecology and Evolution, 18,* 326–330.

Boyd, C., Brooks, T. M., Butchart, S.H.M., Edgar, G. J., da Fonseca, G.A.B., Hawkins, F., Hoffman, M., et al. (2008). Spatial scale and the conservation of threatened species. *Conservation Letters, 1,* 37–43.

Cash, D. W., Adger, W. N., Berkes, F., Garden, P., Lebel, L., Olsson, P., et al. (2006). Scale and cross-scale dynamics: Governance and information in a multilevel world. *Ecology and Society, 11*(2), 8. http://www.ecologyandsociety.org/vol11/iss2/art8/.

Conservation International. (2004). *Conserving Earth's living heritage: A proposed framework for designing biodiversity conservation strategies. Framework document.* Washington, DC: Author.

Eken, G., Bennun, L., Brooks, T. M., Darwall, W., Fishpool, L.D.C., Foster, M. S., et al. (2004). Key biodiversity areas as site conservation targets. *Bioscience, 54,* 1110–1118.

Ferraro, P. J., & Pattanayak, S. K. (2006). Money for nothing? A call for empirical evaluation of biodiversity conservation investments. *PLoS Biology, 4*(4), e105.

Folke, C., Carpenter, C., Elmquist, T., Gunderson, L., Holling, C. S., & Walker, B. (2002). Resilience and sustainable development: Building adaptive capacity in a work of transformations. *Ambio, 31*(5), 437–440.

Langhammer, P. F., Bakarr, M. I., Bennun, L. A., Brooks, T. M., Clay, R. P., Darwall, W., et al. (2007). *Identification and gap analysis of key biodiversity areas: Targets for comprehensive protected area systems.* Gland, Switzerland: International Union for Conservation of Nature.

Lovell, C., Mandondo, A., & Moriarty, P. (2002). The question of scale in integrated natural resource management. *Conservation Ecology, 5*(2), 25. http://www.consecol.org/vol5/iss2/art25/

Mace, G. M., Baillie, J., Masundire, H., Ricketts, T. H., Brooks, T. M., Hoffmann, M., et al. (2005). Biodiversity. In *Millennium Ecosystem Assessment: Current State and Trends: Findings of the Condition and Trends Working Group. Ecosystems and Human Well-being, Vol. 1.* Washington, DC: Island Press.

Noss, R. F. (1990). Indicators for monitoring biodiversity: A hierarchical approach. *Conservation Biology, 4*(4), 355–364.

Poiani, K. A., Richter, B. D., Anderson, M. G., & Richter, H. E. (2000). Biodiversity conservation at multiple scales: Functional sites, landscapes and networks. *BioScience, 50*(2), 133–146.

Pullin, A. S., Knight, T. M., Stone, D. A., & Charman, E. (2004). Do conservation managers use scientific evidence to support their decision-making? *Biological Conservation, 119,* 245–252.

Reid, W. V., Berkes, F., Wilbanks, T., & Capistrano, D. (Eds.). (2006). *Bridging scales and knowledge systems: Linking global science and local knowledge in assessments.* Washington, DC: Millennium Ecosystem Assessment and Island Press.

Royal Society (2003). *Measuring biodiversity for conservation* (Policy document 11/03). Royal Society, London.

ELIZABETH T. KENNEDY, HARI BALASUBRAMANIAN, and WILLIAM E. M. CROSSE are affiliated with Conservation International, where they work on evaluation and monitoring issues.

Hockings, M., Stolton, S., Dudley, N., & James, R. (2009). Data credibility: What are the "right" data for evaluating management effectiveness of protected areas? In M. Birnbaum & P. Mickwitz (Eds.), *Environmental program and policy evaluation: Addressing methodological challenges. New Directions for Evaluation, 122,* 53–63.

5

Data Credibility: What Are the "Right" Data for Evaluating Management Effectiveness of Protected Areas?

Marc Hockings, Sue Stolton, Nigel Dudley, Robyn James

Abstract

Evaluation of protected area management has received increased attention over the past decade, with many thousands of sites assessed. Many of the management effectiveness evaluation systems rely predominantly on expert knowledge and qualitative assessment, especially where the emphasis is on rapid assessment. Others use quantitative data or a mix of data types. We propose that decisions about the appropriateness of qualitative and quantitative data and methods for evaluating management effectiveness of protected areas can be informed by considering issues of (1) the subject matter of evaluation; (2) available resources

Acknowledgments: The generous financial support of the United Nations Foundation for our project work in World Heritage sites is gratefully acknowledged. Many institutions and individuals contributed to the World Heritage project; UNESCO, IUCN, and the various site management agencies and staff in our nine pilot sites are especially thanked. Among many individuals, Natarajan Ishwaran, Marc Patry, Jose Courrau, and Vinod Mathur deserve special mention.

and data; (3) scale, scope, and time frame of the evaluation; and (4) risks asso-ciated with management of the site. © Wiley Periodicals, Inc.

P rotected areas are the cornerstone of efforts to conserve biodiversity and provide associated recreational, economic, and social benefits to humans. The number and total extent of protected areas has been increasing exponentially over the last 50 years, and there are now more than 100,000 protected areas covering some 11% of the earth's land surface (Chape, Harrison, Spalding, & Lysenko, 2005). Yet many sites are under pressure from internal and external threats, and many are degraded (Carey, Dudley, & Stolton, 2000). As Pressman and Wildavsky (1973) illustrated for social pro-grams, government commitment to achievement of specified objectives can be significantly derailed through the implementation process, and the same is true for protected areas as one of the major programs intended to address conservation objectives. Evaluating the effectiveness of management of these sites is one important way of ensuring that the investment of time and effort in establishing and managing protected areas is delivering the benefits that society seeks. Evaluation is also a mechanism for identifying differences in objectives between managers within the administrative agency, surrounding communities, and other stakeholders. The evaluator may not be able to resolve these differences. However, by making them explicit and understand-ing how they relate to the interests, ideologies, knowledge bases, and institu-tional positions of various stakeholders (Weiss, 1995), evaluation may allow policy makers and managers to plan and implement more effective programs.

Evaluation of protected area management effectiveness did not gain real momentum until after the issue was highlighted at the 1992 World Parks Congress in Caracas, Venezuela. Since then, more than 40 methodologies have been developed and applied to assess management effectiveness of protected areas (Leverington, Hockings, & Costa, 2008). Most of the recent systems have been based on the International Union for Conservation of Nature, World Commission on Protected Areas (WCPA) evaluation framework (Hockings et al., 2006). This framework sets out six elements of evaluation with associ-ated criteria used for designing specific evaluation methodologies.

In common with other areas of evaluation (e.g., Attree, 2006), the evi-dence base for conservation practice is not strong (Pullin & Knight, 2005), and planning and decision making frequently rely on qualitative and expe-riential knowledge rather than quantitative data. Concerns have been raised about the use of such data because of questions of consistency and reliabil-ity (Kangas, Alho, Kolehmainen, & Mononen, 1998). Ferraro (elsewhere in this issue) calls for greater reliance on use of empirical data and random-ized control trials in conservation evaluation.

The quantitative versus qualitative debate has a long history in evalu-ation research. This is partly in recognition that a single approach will not suit all circumstances and that the challenge is to match methods to the questions and issues of importance for the case in point (Patton, 1999; see also Margoluis et al. elsewhere in this issue). There is increasing recognition that a combination of both quantitative and qualitative methods can contribute to a single evaluation either by contributing to different stages in the evaluation process or by permitting triangulation of data around an issue within the evaluation process (Sechrest and Sidani, 1995).

Within conservation planning, the lack of comprehensive, consistent, and extensive datasets that could be used for quantitative modeling has led to significant reliance being placed on incorporating expert knowledge into planning decisions (Maddock and Samways, 2000; MacMillan and Marshall, 2005). Many of the protected area management effectiveness evaluation systems such as the World Bank/WWF Management Effectiveness Tracking Tool (Stolton et al., 2007) and the WWF Rapid Appraisal and Prioritization of Protected Area Management (Ervin, 2003) have relied predominantly on expert knowledge and qualitative assessment, especially where the emphasis is on rapid assessment. Reliance on qualitative data has been justified on the basis that capacity and opportunity for more quantitative monitoring and assessment is often limited because costs, in terms of time and expense, are commonly greater for quantitative monitoring. Recently, more quantitative methods for assessing protected area management have also emerged (Dearden and Dempsey, 2004; Venter, Naiman, Biggs, & Pienaar, 2008) and been applied to a limited number of sites.

Concern about the use of qualitative information mostly revolves around issues of reliability and validity, while issues associated with quantitative data relate primarily to concerns about validity, practicality, and cost of collecting data for a large number of sites. Reliability may be a problem with qualitative assessment if experts come to differing conclusions about the aspect of management being evaluated. Validity may be an issue where the state of a single indicator is being used to assess a broader aspect of the protected area (for example, where population data on a few species are taken to indicate overall "health" of an ecosystem), or where quantitative data remain incomplete, as is often the case in protected areas. It is evident to us from discussions with many protected area managers and senior protected area agency staff that the qualitative-quantitative debate is very much on their minds even though it is not set in the context of the wider discussion of this issue occurring in the evaluation literature. Here, we argue that we should learn from the debate in the general evaluation field (Patton, 1999, 2008; Greene, 2007) and frame this discussion in terms of the appropriate application and integration of qualitative and quantitative methods rather than argue for the supremacy of one approach over the other.

Selecting Data Types and Methods for Evaluation

There are a number of issues that need to be addressed when deciding on an evaluation methodology and whether to use qualitative or quantitative data, or a combination of both, in an assessment of protected area management.

We propose that decisions about the appropriateness of qualitative and quantitative data and methods for evaluating management effectiveness of protected areas can be informed by considering issues of (1) the subject matter of evaluation; (2) available resources and data; (3) scale, scope, and time frame of the evaluation; and (4) risks associated with the management of the site.

Subject Matter. The six elements of the WCPA framework (context, planning, inputs, process, outputs, and outcomes) assess aspects of protected area management and consequently address different subject matter. Both qualitative and quantitative data can be used in assessing all the criteria, but some, such as the condition of major values, abatement of threats (both outcome indicators), and implementation of work programs (output indicator), lend themselves to quantitative assessment on the basis of both biophysical and management process monitoring. Others, such as adequacy of engagement with stakeholders (context indicator) and suitability of management processes (a process indicator), are more suited to qualitative assessment by managers and other stakeholders.

Scale and Time Frame. The scale of management effectiveness evaluations varies from single protected areas to whole systems that may include many hundreds of individual sites. Detailed evaluations of management at the site level are commonly focused on enabling an adaptive approach to management and consequent improvements in site management. This does not necessarily favor a preference for quantitative over qualitative data but does place a premium on provision of sufficiently detailed evaluation information (either quantitative or qualitative) to inform site management decisions. In contrast, system-level assessments such as the State of the Parks programs conducted in a number of jurisdictions (Department of Environment and Conservation, NSW, 2005; Gilligan et al., 2005; Parks Victoria, 2007) involving many hundreds of sites are more commonly intended for the purposes of improved accountability and reporting, priority setting, and building community and stakeholder support. In this case, some of the detailed information needed for site-level adaptive management is not required, and assessments with a greater emphasis on qualitative data will be sufficient as long as they meet standards of reliability.

Available Resources and Data. Lack of sufficient funds has been identified as the single most significant impediment to protected area management in global surveys of managers (Hockings et al., 2005; see also Ferraro elsewhere in this issue). Consequently, resources for monitoring and evaluation are severely constrained in most countries. Use of quantitative indicators, especially for assessing the condition of protected area resources and values, will necessitate long-term monitoring to collect data on status and trend for the indicator in question. Such programs are likely to be resource-intensive and beyond the capacity of many protected areas. Monitoring programs are also not attractive for donor funding, where the preference is for short-term projects that will directly affect some aspect of management rather than routine monitoring activities (McShane & Wells, 2004).

Continuity and sustainability are critical issues for both site and system-level assessments, especially when adaptive management is a driving force behind evaluation. We know of a number of instances where ambitious, predominantly quantitative evaluation approaches have been abandoned after a short period because the level of investment in monitoring could not be sustained. Danielsen, Burgess, and Balmford (2005) similarly comment on sustainability problems with biodiversity monitoring programs, especially in developing countries. In most cases, collection of quantitative data will require more time and resources than qualitative assessment, even if rigorous methods of qualitative data collection are used with wide stakeholder involvement and appropriate data triangulation. Using the right mix of qualitative and quantitative methods can help ensure a more sustainable evaluation program. However, we need to pay attention to issues of validity and reliability in assessment because unreliable or invalid assessments are of no use regardless of their sustainability.

Risk. As the "risk" associated with inadequate or incorrect management of a site increases, then the importance of evaluation grows as a means to inform appropriate decision making. This importance of evaluation in turn requires greater attention to data reliability and validity. The issue of risk, as we use the term, relates primarily to four issues:

1. Risk increases as significance of site values increases. If the subject matter being assessed by a specific indicator is of national or global significance, then risk is considered to be high. For example, we might want to assess the condition of a key resource such as the size and health of a population of mountain gorillas. This could involve quantitative monitoring of population numbers of gorillas as well as qualitative assessment of population health by relevant scientists. Because the mountain gorilla is an iconic species and one of the most threatened mammals in the world, the importance of making optimal management decisions for a population is very high.

2. Risk increases as public and political concern or sensitivity increases. Increased scrutiny means that managers will want to have greater confidence in the reliability of assessments to prevent or divert criticism of the evaluation methods and management itself.

3. Risk increases as the significance of decisions arising from the evaluation increases. Significance of decisions will relate to things such as a major change in management policy or major commitments of staff time and funding.

4. Risk increases as uncertainty or ignorance increases. Where our knowledge of the system being managed is poor (i.e., lack of clarity on key values or ecosystem processes), then capacity to target the right indicators to measure is reduced.

As risk increases, it becomes more important than ever to base evaluations on the best data possible. We believe that where the importance of the issue is high, preference should be given either to quantitative indicators where this is possible or to use of more rigorous processes of qualitative data collection by involving participation of relevant experts and stakeholders rather than assessment by a limited number of agency staff. However, it is important to acknowledge that it is impossible to remove all uncertainty from environmental decision making (Constanza & Cornwell, 1992), and there will always be unknown variables and processes operating (Hoffmann-Riem & Wynne, 2002). So although we should strive for the best information, whether we rely on quantitative or qualitative data there will always be aspects not identified or not captured by indicators. Hoffmann-Riem and Wynne (2002) advocate use of multiple perspectives on an issue; wider stakeholder engagement based on different experiences can be useful in pointing out limitations to knowledge.

Case Study: Evaluation of Management Effectiveness in Natural World Heritage Sites

Since 2001 we have been developing and testing a management effectiveness evaluation toolkit in nine natural World Heritage sites in Africa, South Asia, and Latin America (Hockings et al., 2008). The toolkit consists of eleven assessment tools (see Table 5.1) that span the full range of WCPA Management Effectiveness Framework elements. This is one of the most detailed management effectiveness assessment systems applied to protected areas around the world to date. In this case study, we review the choices that we made on the use of either qualitative or quantitative data in relation to the four issues of subject matter, scale, available resources, and risk.

Subject Matter. Assessments that focus on the biophysical, social, and economic resources of the site, particularly the values and objectives, threats, and outcomes for that site (tools 1, 2, and 11), have a primary reliance on quantitative data. For some sites, this involved detailed quantitative monitoring programs for key conservation targets identified to represent each major site value. Alternatively, tools that focus on assessing components of the management system including elements such as involvement of stakeholders and management planning (tools 3, 4, 5, 6, 7, 8, 9, and 10) rely more heavily on qualitative data. Most of these tools depend on the expert judgment of staff (and also stakeholder and expert opinion where relevant) to assess management performance. An exception in this case is tool 10 (work program achievement), which uses quantitative measures of work output.

Scale Time Frame. This evaluation system was developed for implementation at the site rather than system level and with a primary focus on facilitating ongoing, adaptive management. Therefore detailed evaluations using either qualitative or quantitative data were possible. The ongoing nature

Table 5.1. Relative Emphasis on Quantitative and Qualitative Data in the World Heritage Site Evaluation

Assessment Tool	Subject Matter or Indicator	Qualitative	Quantitative
Tool 1: values and objectives	Identification of key site values and objectives, outcomes against which management success will be evaluated	✓✓	✓✓✓
Tool 2: threats	Extent and impact of threats to identified key values	✓	✓✓✓
Tool 3: stakeholders	(1) Stakeholder attributes and interactions; (2) adequacy of stakeholders' engagement	✓✓✓	✓
Tool 4: national context	Adequacy of national environmental policy settings relating to protected areas	✓✓✓	
Tool 5: management planning	Status and adequacy of management planning	✓✓✓	✓
Tool 6: protected area design	Adequacy of design of the PA (size, shape, boundaries, etc.) in relation to biological and social objectives and capacity to effectively manage the site	✓✓✓	✓
Tool 7: resources	Quantity and adequacy of staff, funding, and equipment inputs to PA	✓✓	✓✓
Tool 8: management processes	Performance against standards for PA management processes	✓✓✓	✓
Tool 9: management plan implementation	Extent and trend in implementation of actions prescribed in management plan	✓	✓✓
Tool 10: work program achievement	Extent of achievement against set work program targets	✓	✓✓✓
Tool 11: outcomes of management	(1) Extent to which key values have been maintained or enhanced; (2) extent to which objectives have been achieved	✓✓	✓✓✓

Note: ✓ = minor emphasis on this data type, ✓✓ = moderate emphasis on this data type, ✓✓✓ = major emphasis on this data type.

of the assessments meant that long-term monitoring programs generating quantitative data could be integrated into the evaluation system as required.

Available Resources and Data. All of the pilot sites in the project identified the need for more quantitative monitoring of key biodiversity and other values of the sites, and the project itself was able to go some way toward filling these data gaps (for examples, see the case studies in Hockings et al. 2008). In Serengeti National Park in Tanzania, one of the best researched and most intensively monitored of our project sites, quantitative data were lacking for more than half of the indicators selected to assess the health of the park ecosystems and species. The qualitative component of these assessments can also be significant, especially as comprehensive quantitative data are often hard to acquire. The time and resources needed to organize and conduct stakeholder meetings that allow significant representation and facilitate meaningful input into site management can be expensive for often poorly funded site management agencies.

   Risks. Natural World Heritage sites have been recognized by the international community as flagships for biodiversity conservation. Yet we know that many of these sites are under threat (two of the pilot sites in the case study were on the list of World Heritage in Danger at the commencement of the project). The global significance of these sites, and the international political and public attention that is paid to them, means that risk is high. Two consequences flowed from this assessment. First, where quantitative data are desirable from the perspective of the subject matter of the assessment, then all possible efforts should be expended to acquire these data (although the Serengeti example demonstrates that resource limitations may still restrict available monitoring). Second, attention should be paid to improving the validity and reliability of all evaluation data through adoption of a more rigorous process of assessment and monitoring. For quantitative data, this means attention to monitoring design, sample size, and more rigorous consideration of thresholds. Just as important too is that we must acknowledge that we cannot accurately or adequately monitor everything. The selection of key indicators is paramount, and even then we may still be ignorant of critical issues or the factors contributing to effective management. For qualitative data, it means more attention to incorporation of diverse stakeholder views and more rigorous and in-depth processes of qualitative data collection.

Discussion and Conclusions

Protected area managers and governments are showing increasing interest in evaluating management effectiveness. This is evidenced by the inclusion of management effectiveness evaluation of 30% of the world's protected areas by 2010 as a target within the Convention on Biological Diversity's (CBD) Programme of Work on Protected Areas (Convention on Biological Diversity, 2004). This interest is being translated into action with a growing number of assessments being undertaken around the world. A global study of management effectiveness evaluations undertaken by Leverington, Hockings, and Costa (2008) identified assessments of more than 6,300 protected areas in more than 100 countries, so even though a lot is being done, the remaining task is daunting if the CBD target is going to be met or even closely approached. Collection of quantitative data on all aspects of management across 30% of the world's protected areas (either by number of sites or total area) within a few years is clearly not possible logistically or economically. Using the right mix of qualitative and quantitative data and methods will be important in helping to address the challenge set by the ambitious targets for evaluations.

We have argued that a combination of both quantitative and qualitative methods can and should contribute to evaluation of management effectiveness of a protected area, and that the choice of data depends on some key factors:

- What element of management is being assessed (i.e., subject matter)
- The level at which the assessment is being undertaken (i.e., either a single protected area or a protected area system)
- The resources available, in the short and long run
- The degree of reliability required depending on the significance of the element being assessed and the risk involved

This combination of qualitative and quantitative methods is in accord with Greene's call for methodological pluralism (2007). The quality of the evaluation depends not on whether qualitative or quantitative data are used but on the use of appropriate assessment processes. As demands for precision and reliability in protected area evaluation increase, it is important to place emphasis on using the most appropriate data collection and assessment process. A good process is the critical factor, rather than just a preference for quantitative over qualitative data.

Our experience in the World Heritage case study also highlighted the importance of process use of evaluations. Evaluation capacity building within the site management organizations was a significant outcome in all cases. At least four of the five types of process use identified by Forss, Rebien, & Carlsson (2002) were evident in our case study: strengthening organizational learning, building professional networks and strengthening partnerships, creating shared understanding, and strengthening management (see case studies in Chapter 4 of Hockings et al., 2008, for examples). Incorporating qualitative data such as the experience and knowledge of managers and stakeholders was a critical element in generating these process use benefits.

References

Attree, M. (2006). Evaluating healthcare education: Issues and methods. *Nurse Education Today, 26,* 640–646.

Carey, C., Dudley, N., & Stolton, S. (2000). *Squandering paradise? The importance and vulnerability of the world's protected areas.* Gland, Switzerland: WWF.

Chape, S., Harrison, J., Spalding, M., & Lysenko, I. (2005). Measuring the extent and effectiveness of protected areas as an indicator for meeting global biodiversity targets.

NEW DIRECTIONS FOR EVALUATION • DOI: 10.1002/ev

Philosophical Transactions of the Royal Society B-Biological Sciences, 360(1454), 443–455.

Constanza, R., & Cornwell, L. (1992). The 4P approach to dealing with scientific uncertainty. *Environment, 34*(9), 12.

Convention on Biological Diversity. (2004). Programme of work on protected areas. Retrieved September 29, 2006, from http://www.biodiv.org/decisions/default.aspx?dec=VII/28

Danielsen, F., Burgess, N. D., & Balmford, A. (2005). Monitoring matters: Examining the potential of locally-based approaches. *Biodiversity and Conservation, 14*(11), 2507–2542.

Dearden, P., & Dempsey, J. (2004). Protected areas in Canada: Decade of change. *Canadian Geographer-Geographe Canadien, 48*(2), 225–239.

Department of Environment and Conservation, NSW. (2005). *State of the parks 2004.* Sydney, Australia, Department of Environment and Conservation.

Ervin, J. (2003). *WWF Rapid Assessment and Prioritization of Protected Area Management (RAPPAM) methodology.* Gland, Switzerland: WWF.

Forss, K., Rebien, C., & Carlsson, J. (2002). Process use of evaluations: Types of use that precede lessons learned and feedback. *Evaluation, 8*(1), 29–45.

Gilligan, B., Dudley, N., de Tejada, A. F., & Toivonen, H. (2005). Management effectiveness evaluation of Finland's protected areas. Finland: Metsähallitus.

Greene, J. (2007). *Mixing methods in social inquiry.* San Francisco: Jossey-Bass.

Hockings, M., Machlis, G., Nielsen, E., Russel, K., Nyambe, N., & James, R. (2005). *Delegate Survey Report, Fifth World Parks Congress 2003.* IUCN, WCPA and University of Queensland, St Lucia, Australia.

Hockings, M., Stolton, S., Dudley, N., James, R., Mathur, V., Courrau, J., et al. (2008). *Enhancing our Heritage Toolkit: Assessing management effectiveness of natural World Heritage sites* (World Heritage Papers No. 23). Paris: UNESCO World Heritage Centre.

Hockings, M., Stolton, S., Leverington, F., Dudley, N., & Courrau, J. (2006). *Evaluating effectiveness: A framework for assessing management effectiveness of protected areas* (2nd ed.). Gland, Switzerland: IUCN.

Hoffmann-Riem, H., & Wynne, B. 2002. In risk assessment, one has to admit ignorance: Explaining there are things we can't know could improve public confidence in science. *Nature, 416*, 123.

Kangas, J., Alho, J., Kolehmainen, O., & Mononen, A. (1998). Analyzing consistency of experts' judgments: Case of assessing forest biodiversity. *Forest Science, 44*(4), 610–617.

Leverington, F., Hockings, M., & Costa, K. L. (2008). *Management effectiveness evaluation in protected areas: Report for the project Global Study into Management Effectiveness Evaluation of Protected Areas.* Brisbane, Australia: University of Queensland, IUCN WCPA, TNC, WWF.

MacMillan, D. C., & Marshall, K. (2005). The Delphi process: An expert-based approach to ecological modeling in data poor environments. *Animal Conservation, 9*, 11–19.

Maddock, A. H., & Samways, M. J. (2000). Planning for biodiversity conservation based on the knowledge of biologists. *Biodiversity and Conservation, 9*(8), 1153–1169.

McShane, T., & Wells, M. (Eds.). (2004). *Getting biodiversity projects to work: Towards more effective conservation and development.* New York: Columbia University Press.

Parks Victoria. (2007). *Victoria's State of the Parks Report.* Melbourne: Author.

Patton, M. Q. (1999). Enhancing the quality and credibility of qualitative analysis. *Health Services Research, 34*(5 Part II), 1189–1208.

Patton, M. Q. (2008). *Utilization-focused evaluation.* Los Angeles: Sage.

Pressman, J. L., & Wildavsky, A. B. (1973). *Implementation: How great expectations in Washington are dashed in Oakland.* Berkeley: University of California Press.

Pullin, A. S., & Knight, T. M. (2005). Assessing conservation management's evidence base: A survey of management-plan compilers in the United Kingdom and Australia. *Conservation Biology, 19*(6), 1989–1996.

Sechrest, L., & Sidani, S. (1995). Quantitative and qualitative methods. *Evaluation and Program Planning, 18*(1), 77–87.

Stolton, S., Hockings, M., Dudley, N., MacKinnon, K., Whitten, T., & Leverington, F. (2007). *Reporting progress in protected areas: A site-level management effectiveness tracking tool.* Gland, Switzerland: World Bank/WWF Alliance for Forest Conservation and Sustainable Use.

Venter, F. J., Naiman, R. J., Biggs, H. C., & Pienaar, D. J. (2008). The evolution of conservation management philosophy: Science, environmental change and social adjustments in Kruger National Park. *Ecosystems, 11*(2), 173–192.

Weiss, C. H. (1995). The four "I's" of school reform: How interests, ideology, information, and institution affect teachers and principals. *Harvard Educational Review, 65*(4), 571–592.

MARC HOCKINGS *is affiliated with the School of Integrative Systems at University of Queensland, Australia.*

SUE STOLTON *and* NIGEL DUDLEY *are affiliated with Equilibrium Research, Bristol, United Kingdom.*

ROBYN JAMES *is affiliated with the School of Integrative Systems at University of Queensland, Australia.*

Pullin, A. S., & Knight, T. M. (2009). Data credibility: A perspective from systematic reviews in environmental management. In M. Birnbaum & P. Mickwitz (Eds.), *Environmental program and policy evaluation: Addressing methodological challenges. New Directions for Evaluation, 122,* 65–74.

6

Data Credibility: A Perspective From Systematic Reviews in Environmental Management

Andrew S. Pullin, Teri M. Knight

Abstract

To use environmental program evaluation to increase effectiveness, predictive power, and resource allocation efficiency, evaluators need good data. Data require sufficient credibility in terms of fitness for purpose and quality to develop the necessary evidence base. The authors examine elements of data credibility using experience from critical appraisal of studies on environmental interventions employing systematic review methodology. They argue that critical appraisal of methodological quality is a key skill to improve both retrospective evaluation and prospective planning of monitoring of environmental programs. Greater transparency and data sharing among evaluators could facilitate rapid development in approaches to environmental evaluation that improve data credibility. © Wiley Periodicals, Inc.

If we want to know what works and what doesn't, we collect data and analyze them. But the confidence with which we can interpret those data in the context of our questions depends on their quality and the strength of the evidence they provide (how credible they are). Is the measured effect

real, and can we attribute the outcome to the interventions we have put in place? Data credibility is just as important for monitoring and evaluation as it is in experimental manipulation and interpretation: to ensure that both accuracy and reliability are accepted by both evaluators and other stakeholders, to demonstrate improved performance of environmental programs, and to show that money has been effectively used to produce environmental benefits.

To professional evaluators, the generic issues of experimental design and data credibility will be familiar and have been covered elsewhere (Donaldson & Christie, 2005; Julnes and Rog, 2007). The purpose of this chapter is to discuss the issue of data credibility, specifically as it relates to environmental data, and to explore its importance to outcome evaluation (often also called impact evaluation) of environmental programs. We approach environmental programs as complex interventions and consider the problem of data credibility from an evidence-based perspective (Pullin & Knight, 2001). Evaluating effectiveness of commonly used single interventions and relating it to the success of more complex programs is now routine in some sectors such as the health services. However, data generation in human health disciplines is highly regulated in terms of the quality of methodology and the definition of outcome measures, compared to the field of environmental management. As a result, it is common to assume that the nature of the wider environment presents novel challenges in terms of data generation and interpretation. We argue here that the challenges are not novel; they are simply bigger and we can therefore build on the experiences of other sectors, learning from the application of systematic review methodologies, first developed within health care, to environmental interventions.

Credible data are both "fit for purpose" and of high quality. We focus on a number of key components of data credibility, exploring a broad range of data issues, none of which is unique to environmental management but many of which are aggravated by the challenges of measuring change in specific components of complex environmental systems. We advocate use of critical appraisal of data as employed in systematic review methodology to assess quality of data and fitness for purpose. Using a series of case studies, this chapter demonstrates how systematic review methodology has developed in the field of environmental management to address problems of data credibility.

Critical Appraisal of Data and Systematic Review Methodology

The process of systematic review is becoming widely used and developed as a tool for assessing effectiveness of interventions in environmental management (Pullin & Knight, 2001). The specific questions addressed by systematic reviews usually concern the assessment of effectiveness or impacts of various kinds of interventions. In other words, How effective is the intervention in achieving specific goals? In this way, it is very similar to outcome (impact) evaluation. The methodology attempts to gather together and synthesize all data of relevance to the review question. It is therefore retrospective, but problems encountered in retrospective appraisal of data sets can act as valuable pointers for future experimental design. The methodology is considered rigorous, objective, and transparent and specifically attempts to minimize error and bias as well as maximize analytical power.

The relevance of systematic review to program evaluation and to the problem of data credibility lies in the critical appraisal of data that forms a central pillar of systematic review (Pullin & Stewart, 2006). In critically appraising the data from individual studies, we examine the two main aspects of data credibility: fitness for purpose and data quality. These two components are often interrelated, but essentially fitness for purpose concerns the extent to which the objectives and design of the studies are likely to address the review question, whereas appraisal of data quality looks at how the methods employed in the study attempt to minimize error and bias.

In undertaking the first systematic reviews in the environmental field, it has become evident that, along with the accessibility of data, the quality of methodology used to generate primary data is a major barrier to evaluation of interventions (Stewart, Coles, & Pullin, 2005). Both are notably inferior compared to some other sectors such as the health services. Accessibility of data is improving and is being tackled on a number of fronts, but increased attention needs to be paid to the data quality issue (Sutherland, Pullin, Dolman, & Knight, 2004).

Error and Bias

The twin threats of error and bias are ever present in study designs and encourage misinterpretation. Poor design can lead to inappropriate measures of outcomes and insufficient power for rigorous evaluation. Arguably this problem is greater in environmental management than in most other sectors. Collection, management, and analysis of raw data and constructed statistics create severe challenges in the field of environmental management, whether one is undertaking pure research or monitoring and evaluation. There are few sufficiently rigorous standards in place to ensure that data are collected uniformly (Ferraro & Pattanayak, 2006). Transparency of monitoring protocols is frequently lacking. At worst this problem results in unreliable data sets with questionable statistics for assessing environmental dimensions. The problem is often exacerbated by inadequate funds and unrealistically rapid assessments resulting from monitoring's low-priority ranking, leading to lack of strength in the evidence base. This problem grows to a greater magnitude when attempts are made to synthesize beyond one project site through meta-analyses and multisite evaluations. Synthesizing data from multiple sites may increase statistical power, but it does not eliminate error and bias. Although this problem is not unique to the environmental field, the training of practitioners in the natural sciences leads to significant challenges in the perceptions of the need for collection and use of different types of data.

In the health services, a hierarchy of research is recognized in critical appraisal that assigns a comparative value to the data in terms of the scientific rigor of the methodology used (Stevens & Milne, 1997). The hierarchy of methodology can be viewed as generic and has been transferred from medicine to ecology and environmental management (Pullin & Knight, 2003). Many systematic reviews in medicine include only evidence generated through randomized controlled trials (RCTs), especially at latter stages of developing an intervention. Other methodologies are viewed as more prone to error and bias and thus less credible. Where a number of well-designed, high-quality studies are available, others with inferior methodology may therefore be rejected entirely. Alternatively, the effects of individual studies can be weighted according to their position in the "quality hierarchy." Sensitivity analyses are often employed to assess the impact of including and excluding lower-quality data. Of course, even high-quality designs can result in poor-quality data if not well implemented.

The RCT gold standard of methodological quality is rare in environmental monitoring and evaluation. This gives environmental evaluators two basic options: (1) make RCTs more common, that is, find ways of increasing the credibility of data being generated by setting higher standards in experimentation and monitoring (see Ferraro in this issue); or (2) use variable-quality data sets in ever more sophisticated ways that account for error and bias (see Hockings et al. in this issue). Either way, we need to understand the problems posed by differential methodological quality.

Susceptibility to bias is generally accepted as the main driver of methodological quality. The quality of a research design can be judged by the extent to which it minimizes susceptibility to these biases. Selection bias is probably the greatest threat to data credibility in program evaluation because of the difficulty of randomization of treatment and control. Experimenter error is a much more varied problem that is largely outside the scope of this chapter, but the high risk of sampling error (sampling a subset that is unrepresentative of the whole) is also minimized by the high-quality designs having sufficient sample size.

Pseudoreplication

Another role of critical appraisal of methodological quality, one that is especially important in environment studies, is to check for pseudoreplication. Programs are often implemented at single sites, and evaluating effectiveness often involves multiple sampling from that site, together with a control site. In analyzing the effectiveness of that individual program, it is perfectly valid to compare the treatment and control means and variances of those multiple samples. However, when synthesizing data from multiple sites to address a more global question of effectiveness, using multiple samples from one site as if they were independent is invalid. This is termed pseudoreplication and is usually detectable through critical appraisal, but it is otherwise often overlooked and thus common in the peer-reviewed literature.

An example of this comes from a systematic review of the effectiveness of temperate marine reserves for conserving biodiversity. Of the 34 studies identified, 31 presented repeated observation on the same areas and were therefore pseudoreplicated when synthesizing data across reserves (Stewart et al., 2008). The simple solution to pseudoreplication is to aggregate data at the site level. However, this often reduces sample size to a critically low level for statistical analysis. The more important implication for single program evaluations is to beware of nonindependence of data points, reducing sample size to a level that prevents meaningful statistical analysis.

Fitness for Purpose: Context, Attribution, and Effect Modifiers

Systematic reviews aim to assess the effectiveness of an intervention by drawing together data from individual studies. Through critical appraisal, we assess the credibility of the data generated by each study, within the context in which they are measured. In the social sciences, synthesis of findings or generalizations concerning the effectiveness of interventions may be considered inappropriate if the context within which the intervention is applied is a key determining factor of outcome (Guba & Lincoln, 1989; Pawson & Tilley, 1997). The ability to assess the impact of context on effectiveness of the intervention depends on its complexity and the extent to which its critical components are understood and measured. For example, a systematic review on in-stream devices synthesized data on outcome (salmonid abundance) but was also able to explore the impact on those outcomes of "effect modifiers," such as stream size and flow rate (Stewart et al., 2009). These were the critical components of context in this case. Thus, when adequately controlled for, or measured across many studies, an understanding of effect modifiers can be fundamental to predicting effectiveness of an intervention under different environmental conditions (contexts).

Increasingly, environmental management interventions are involving strategies targeting human behavior as intermediate outcomes for mitigating stressors to an ecosystem, and these will obviously have more complex contexts, which may not be fully amenable to simple measurement and statistical analysis. It would, though, still be important for critical components of the context within which the interventions took place to be explored and described as fully as possible so that the findings of systematic review can be presented against that contextual background.

Clearly, identification and measurement of contextual factors within research studies will improve the generalizability of the findings of systematic review of effectiveness of interventions to other contexts. However, generation of credible data is a first step to testing the effect of context; thus even though this issue may be important, we have yet to reach a stage with environmental data where a debate can be held about what works for whom and in what circumstances (Pawson & Tilley, 1997).

Consideration of effect modifiers is also important in another key problem for program evaluation, that of attribution. In considering a large and complex program, how can we attribute the observed outcome to the existence of the program, in the presence of many potential effect modifiers—other environmental and socioeconomic variables that may be causing change—in the ecological target of study? This is perhaps the most straightforward example of where high-quality data sets can allow an evaluator to address the problem, whereas low-quality data have little or no value. Here we are looking for study designs that not only limit error and bias for attribution but also measure other key variables (effect modifiers) to explain heterogeneity in outcome. For example, a systematic review of the effectiveness of the herbicide asulam for control of bracken, *Pteridium aquilinum,* was able to show evidence of effectiveness but also deal with some problems of effect modifiers such as timing and frequency of application (Stewart et al., 2007). Fifteen independent data points were available from randomized controlled trials testing the effectiveness of asulam. These data suggest that repeated application is necessary to achieve effective control, thus revealing information of added value beyond the simple question of its effectiveness.

Fitness for Purpose: Variable Outcomes Measures

Once data of adequate quality have been selected, the issue of variable outcome measures can become problematic. It is often the case that studies use different outcome measures such that not all may be equally relevant to the review question. Commonly, when multiple studies are being considered, data will often differ in the temporal and spatial scales employed (see Kennedy et al., elsewhere in this issue). What to measure over what spatial and temporal scales is rarely standardized in environmental management. Synthesizing evidence on the effectiveness of engineered in-stream devices for the management of salmonid populations, Stewart et al. (2009) found it necessary to distinguish between measures of change in overall population size estimated at the "reach" scale and measures of change in the aggregation of individuals in the vicinity of devices. Interpretation of effectiveness can therefore rest on decisions about which outcome data are most credible.

Fitness for Purpose: Internal Versus External Validity

There are dangers in rigid application of a quality hierarchy in ecology and environmental management (Pullin & Stewart, 2006). A rigorous methodology, such as a randomized controlled trial, is normally viewed as superior thanks to its ability to minimize error and bias, but in reality many RCTs may achieve this high internal validity in terms of experimental design at the expense of external validity (its approximation to the real field situation). This can be manifest as experimental application over a short time period and small spatial scale when effects might only be detectable over a longer period and at a larger scale. A site comparison over a longer time series might have greater external validity even though it lacks randomization and large sample size.

Effectiveness of control methods for the invasive shrub *Rhododendron ponticum* is highly contentious. Evidence for the effectiveness of the commonly used herbicide metsulfuron methyl comes from pot-based studies undertaken in glasshouses (Tyler et al., 2006). These studies have reasonable internal validity, but other studies undertaken in the field cast some doubt on the effectiveness of this intervention, suggesting that the glasshouse experiments lack external validity. The converse of this situation also exists in this case, with a collection of single observations of practitioners following their *Rhododendron* control efforts. Here there may be high external validity, but with small sample sizes and no control group, resulting in a study with low internal validity. Either way, the data should be considered as having low credibility.

In synthesizing data sets where internal or external validity problems are suspected, more pragmatic quality weightings and judicious use of sensitivity analysis (including and excluding studies to assess their influence on the overall outcome) can be employed to explore the extent of the data credibility problem.

Qualitative Versus Quantitative Data: An Issue of Both Fitness for Purpose and Data Quality

Both quantitative and qualitative methods can and should contribute to the evaluation of an intervention. Addressing data credibility is as essential for qualitative data as it is for quantitative. The issue of fitness for purpose applies to both. For example, in public health, outcome evaluation of a program designed to support people in quitting smoking may want not only to count the number of people who quit during the intervention but also to understand how the experience of the intervention and of quitting smoking affected health and perceived well-being. Qualitative research methods could be appropriately used for this purpose alongside quantitative measures. However, in relation to fitness for purpose, it is less likely in environment management than in health research that qualitative data will be suitable for assessing long-term biological or ecological outcomes (usually one cannot ask the subjects to join a focus group). We will most probably be looking for quantitative outcome indicators, for example measures of frequency or abundance.

Systematic review methodology is now developing "mixed method" approaches whereby both quantitative and qualitative data are being used to examine effectiveness of interventions (Newton, Stewart, Diaz, Golicher, & Pullin, 2007). Different sets of criteria are used to critically appraise the methodological quality of several types of studies; how we assess rigor is different from quantitative data but just as important for qualitative data. We should check that explicit systematic methods have been used to draw conclusions and to test them for both quantitative and qualitative data. These methods should be credible, dependable, and replicable, in either qualitative or quantitative terms (Miles & Huberman, 1994).

Qualitative research can be conducted in many ways, following established research traditions, and ways of analyzing qualitative data are continuously evolving (as they are with quantitative data). Conducting good qualitative research can be as time-consuming and resource-intensive as methods that produce quantitative data (Miles & Huberman, 1994). We should be careful to check that qualitative data used in an evaluation actually satisfy data quality criteria, and are not just "words" collected in some undefined way following poor-quality methodology. Where program evaluators have "for reasons of resource constraint" used qualitative data instead of collecting the required quantitative data, we should satisfy ourselves that these data are fit for purpose and of acceptable quality. (For more information on this topic, see Hockings elsewhere in this issue.)

Improving Data Credibility

An obvious solution to improving data credibility is to improve the methodological standards required for environmental monitoring and evaluation. If good planning ensures that the right processes are put in place from the beginning, then evaluation should in turn be more rigorous (Margoluis & Salafsky, 1998). This key point is also addressed by Margoluis, Stem, and colleagues elsewhere in this issue.

Careful assessment is needed of choice of methodology and agreement reached on an appropriate strength of evidence required. Such choices depend on the likely costs of being wrong in acting, or in not acting, to stop or continue the intervention (Gee, 2008). Choosing an appropriate strength of evidence involves trade-offs. If the risk of getting it wrong is very high (i.e., we are dealing with an endangered species), then recognizing that we have no credible data on outcomes might be better than using data to make decisions that are not relevant and may be subject to unknown biases and inaccuracies (Ferraro & Pattanayak, 2006; see also Hockings et al. elsewhere in this issue).

Given that we have guidance on achieving high-quality methodological standards, the question becomes how we drive up those standards. High methodological standards are maintained in the health services partly as a result of the presence of ethical committees. These are independent bodies that review proposals for clinical trials and the like. A key function of such bodies is to ensure that the study design and monitoring methods are adequate to evaluate the effectiveness of the intervention. Not to be risking harm and wasting money could also be seen as an ethical issue in an environmental context. Should we not ensure that interventions designed to conserve biodiversity are monitored using methodology adequate to evaluate whether the resources expended are doing more good than harm? How this would operate in the relatively unregulated world of environmental management is uncertain, but program donors must have a key responsibility (and vested interest) to ensure that scarce resources are used ethically.

A key function of retrospective evaluation is to increase our predictive power so that future resources can be better allocated. Two final lessons from systematic review and evidence-based practice, concerning transparency and data sharing, relate directly to this function. First, future resource allocation decisions concerning future environmental programs will be informed by current evaluations only if the data are shared and the evaluation process is transparent. Proper reporting of methodology aids appraisal of quality. Systematic reviews are designed to be transparent and repeatable, and it would help if program evaluation methods were equally so. Second, the philosophy of evidence-based practice is to share knowledge and realize the potential of data (with caveats concerning data protection when appropriate). This also means sharing problems of credibility and finding solutions. Using lessons learned from systematic review in the environmental field could help address data credibility problems and help guide future program evaluation.

References

Donaldson, S. I., & Christie, C. A. (2005). The 2004 Claremont Debate: Lipsey vs. Scriven—Determining causality in program evaluation and applied research: Should experimental evidence be the gold standard? *Journal of MultiDisciplinary Evaluation, 3*, 60–77.

Ferraro, P. J., & Pattanayak, S. K. (2006). Money for nothing? A call for empirical evaluation of biodiversity conservation investments. *PloS Biology, 4*, 482–488.

Gee, D. (2008). Establishing evidence for early action: The prevention of reproductive and developmental harm. *Basic and Clinical Pharmacology and Toxicology, 102*, 257–266.

Guba, E. G., & Lincoln, Y. S. (1989). *Fourth generation evaluation*. Newbury Park, CA: Sage.

Julnes, G., & Rog, D. J. (Eds.) (2007). Informing federal policies on evaluation methodology: Building the evidence base for method choice in government sponsored evaluation. *New Directions for Evaluation, 113.*

Margoluis, R., & Salafsky, N. (1998). *Measures of success: Designing, managing and monitoring conservation and development projects*. University of Michigan: Island Press.

Miles, M. B., & Huberman, A. M. (1994). *Qualitative data analysis* (2nd ed.). London: Sage.

Newton, A. C., Stewart, G. B, Diaz, A., Golicher, D., & Pullin, A. S. (2007). Bayesian belief networks as a tool for evidence-based conservation management. *Journal for Nature Conservation, 15*, 144–160.

Pawson, R., & Tilley, N. (1997). *Realistic evaluation*. London: Sage.

Pullin, A. S., & Knight, T. M. (2001). Effectiveness in conservation practice: Pointers from medicine and public health. *Conservation Biology, 15*, 50–54.

Pullin, A. S., & Knight, T. M. (2003). Support for decision making in conservation practice: An evidence-based approach. *Journal for Nature Conservation, 11*, 83–90.

Pullin, A. S., & Stewart, G. B. (2006). Guidelines for systematic review in conservation and environmental management. *Conservation Biology, 20*, 1647–1656.

Stevens, A., & Milne, R. (1997). The effectiveness revolution and public health. In G. Scally (Ed.), *Progress in public health* (pp. 197–225). London: Royal Society for Medicine Press.

Stewart, G. B., Bayliss, H. R., Showler, D. A., Sutherland, W. J., & Pullin, A. S. (2009). Effectiveness of engineered in-stream structure mitigation measures for increasing salmonid abundance: A systematic review. *Ecological Applications, 19*, 931–941.

Stewart, G. B., Coles, C. F., & Pullin, A. S. (2005). Applying evidence-based practice in conservation management: Lessons from the first systematic review and dissemination projects. *Biological Conservation, 126*, 270–278.

Stewart, G. B., Côté, I. M., Kaiser, M. J., Halpern, B. S., Lester, S. E., Bayliss, H. R., et al. (2008). Are marine protected areas effective tools for sustainable fisheries management? I. Biodiversity impact of marine reserves in temperate zones. *Systematic Review* No. 23. Retrieved April 22, 2009, from http://www.environmentalevidence.org.

Stewart, G. B., Pullin, A. S., & Tyler, C. (2007). The effectiveness of asulam for bracken (*Pteridium aquilinum*) control in the United Kingdom: A meta-analysis. *Environmental Management, 40*, 747–760.

Sutherland, W. J., Pullin, A. S., Dolman, P. M., & Knight, T. M. (2004). The need for evidence-based conservation. *Trends in Ecology and Evolution, 19*, 305–308.

Tyler, C., Pullin, A. S., & Stewart, G. B. (2006). Effectiveness of management interventions to control invasion by *Rhododendron ponticum*. *Environmental Management, 37*, 513–522.

ANDREW S. PULLIN *is a professor and* TERI M. KNIGHT *is a research fellow at the Centre for Evidence-Based Conservation, School of the Environment and Natural Resources, Bangor University, United Kingdom.*

NEW DIRECTIONS FOR EVALUATION • DOI: 10.1002/ev

Ferraro, P. J. (2009). Counterfactual thinking and impact evaluation in environmental policy. In M. Birnbaum & P. Mickwitz (Eds.), *Environmental program and policy evaluation: Addressing methodological challenges. New Directions for Evaluation, 122*, 75–84.

7

Counterfactual Thinking and Impact Evaluation in Environmental Policy

Paul J. Ferraro

Abstract

Impact evaluations assess the degree to which changes in outcomes can be attributed to an intervention rather than to other factors. Such attribution requires knowing what outcomes would have looked like in the absence of the intervention. This counterfactual world can be inferred only indirectly through evaluation designs that control for confounding factors. Some have argued that environmental policy is different from other social policy fields, and thus attempting to establish causality through identification of counterfactual outcomes is quixotic. This chapter argues that elucidating causal relationships through counterfactual thinking and experimental or quasi-experimental designs is absolutely critical in environmental policy, and that many opportunities for doing so exist. Without more widespread application of such approaches, little progress will be made on building the evidence base in environmental policy. © Wiley Periodicals, Inc.

In presentations on evaluation to environmental scientists and field practitioners, I often begin by describing a Florida conservation education program that was designed to reduce residential outdoor water use (Mulville-Friel & Anderson, 1996). The program was piloted in a neighborhood where outdoor water consumption was measured before and after

the program. After program implementation, mean household water consumption declined 29%. The effort was expanded to another neighborhood where water consumption declined 38%.

Most audience members indicate that a program officer would be justified in broadly scaling up the education program. In their eyes, the evaluation strategy has the required attributes to credibly evaluate program effectiveness: a clear theory of change and a specific and measurable outcome indicator observed before and after the intervention. They also indicate that the quality of the program's evidence is much better than in many environmental programs. Environmental programs often lack clear theories of causal relationships and baseline indicators. I end the Florida example by asking audience members what they would think about the evidence of program effectiveness if I told them (truthfully) that rainfall had increased at the time when the program was expanded to a second community, and that water consumption declined 31% in a nearby community that received no education. They immediately realize that the original evaluation design was missing important elements.

Impact evaluations assess the degree to which changes in outcomes can be attributed to a program, policy, or intervention "treatment," rather than to confounding factors that also affect the outcomes. Impact evaluations answer the question, "Does the intervention work better than no intervention at all (or a proposed alternative intervention)?" An answer requires knowing what outcomes would have looked like in the absence of the intervention. This counterfactual world, however, can be inferred only indirectly. Efforts to measure causes of environmental outcomes through counterfactual thinking are rare in the environmental literature.

In this chapter, I argue that counterfactual thinking is critical to building the evidence base in environmental policy about what types of interventions work and under what conditions. More specifically, I argue that:

- Much of what is called evaluation of environmental program impact is simply monitoring of indicators
- Counterfactual thinking is essential to drawing inferences about program effectiveness because realistic behavioral theories typically yield ambiguous predictions about environmental program impacts, and because environmental outcomes are affected by many confounding factors correlated with the timing and location of interventions
- Advancing counterfactual thinking through experimental and quasi-experimental designs faces the same barriers that exist in other social policy fields, but these barriers are particularly pervasive in environmental policy
- In comparison to other social policy fields, there are few examples of experimental or quasi-experimental evaluations
- Despite the barriers and paucity of examples, there are substantial opportunities to elucidate causal relationships through experimental and quasi-experimental designs

NEW DIRECTIONS FOR EVALUATION • DOI: 10.1002/ev

The Need for Counterfactual Thinking in Environmental Policy Evaluation

The environmental literature is replete with data on biophysical processes and status indicators. Yet when evaluating how environmental policies and programs affect these processes and indicators, the literature lags behind other social policy fields, such as public health and poverty reduction. For example, a global ecosystem assessment (Millennium Ecosystem Assessment) contained hundreds of pages of data to support its characterization of the state of the world's ecosystems. However, one of its "main messages" (MA, 2005, p. 122) is that "few well-designed empirical analyses assess even the most common biodiversity conservation measures." Others have made similar arguments in the case of ecosystem conservation (Pullin & Knight, 2001; Sutherland, Pullin, Dolman, & Knight, 2004; Saterson et al., 2004; Stem, Margoluis, Salafsky, & Brown, 2005; Ferraro & Pattanayak, 2006), energy conservation (Frondel & Schmidt, 2005), and pollution policy (Bennear & Coglianese, 2005; Greenstone & Gayer, 2007).

Much of the emphasis to date has been on monitoring: collecting data on indicators of status and trend, such as pollution levels, habitat areas, and management effectiveness scores. Indicators are important because they allow us to document progress toward policy goals. They can reveal if more action is needed to achieve a goal. Alone, however, they cannot reveal if an intervention affected progress toward that goal.

Environmental scientists and practitioners often assume that evaluation is simply the act of taking a careful look at the monitoring data. If the indicator improves, a program is deemed to be "working." If the indicator worsens, one infers the program is "failing." In contrast, impact evaluation contrasts changes in an indicator to some estimate of the counterfactual change in the indicator, the change that would have occurred without program. The essence of counterfactual thinking is elimination of plausible rival interpretations of observed outcomes.

Hidden Biases in Environmental Program Evaluation

Eliminating plausible rival interpretations of observed outcomes requires complex theories. Theories have power in the degree to which they exclude what one can observe and still find the theory to be correct. Demonstrating that no plausible alternative theories can account for what has been observed is important in counterfactual analyses. Theory alone, however, is not sufficient to identify impacts.

Realistic theories of behavioral change in environmental contexts are often consistent with positive, negative, and neutral program impacts. For example, interventions to induce firms and citizens to adopt energy-efficient technologies in order to lower energy consumption and thereby reduce greenhouse gas emissions (IPCC, 2007) may achieve the opposite, particularly in low-income nations (see special issues of *Energy Policy* and *Energy and Environment*, 2000). Although efficient technologies reduce the energy consumption per unit of power, heating, cooling, or lighting, they also reduce the effective price of these outputs and thus increase demand (thermostat settings change, lights stay on longer). Complex potential responses are common in environmental programs that use regulations, incentives, or education (information). Thus the extent to which many environmental programs have the desired effect is an empirical question.

Empirical analyses, however, are made difficult by pervasive confounding factors that mask program failure or mimic program success. This includes (1) cotemporaneous factors that are correlated with the treatment intervention and outcomes; and (2) selection bias, where treated units are selected, or select themselves, to receive the intervention on the basis of characteristics that also affect the outcome. These sources of confounding factors are found in nearly all environmental programs, and predicting their direction and magnitude ex ante is difficult. This in turn confounds efforts at credible ex post impact evaluations.

With regard to cotemporaneous confounding factors, a large set of factors, including changes in weather and in relative prices and other economic characteristics (such as fuel prices or employment opportunities), affect environmental outcomes. Comparing outcomes in the treatment group to outcomes in a control group can reduce bias from cotemporaneous confounders, but pervasive selection bias implies that the outcome of the average untreated observation will rarely represent the counterfactual outcome of the average treated observation. For example, the characteristics that lead program administrators to target certain individuals, firms, species, or areas are frequently correlated with outcomes (see Figure 7.1). Voluntary programs also suffer from self-selection bias. For example, incentive programs (payments for environmental services, eco-labeling, adoption of environmental management systems) often reward people or firms for not engaging in environmentally destructive activities that, at many places and times, would not be done even in the absence of the program.

To distinguish between program effects and hidden biases, counterfactual thinking is absolutely essential. To engage in such thinking, analysts often collect data within quasi-experimental and experimental designs. These designs attempt to identify exogenous variation in the program in order to identify its impact. Greenstone and Gayer (2007) argue that the field of environmental policy is "flush with opportunities to apply these techniques." In the next section, I demonstrate that there are indeed opportunities for applying these designs.

Nevertheless, such designs are much rarer in environmental policy than in other social policy fields. Their rarity arises from environmental practitioners and scientists' lack of familiarity with appropriate designs and methods, as well as barriers to doing *any* environmental program impact evaluation, whether through experimental or nonexperimental designs.

Figure 7.1.   Experimental and Quasi-Experimental Designs in Environmental Program Evaluation

How much do indoor air pollution reductions affect infant and mother's health? Households that invest to improve indoor air quality also tend to be wealthier, be better informed, and have greater concerns about their health. To address potential confounders, the RESPIRE study (Diaz et al., 2007) randomly provided less-polluting cook stoves to women with children. Women and children in the treatment group experienced substantial reductions in carbon monoxide exposure and reported poor health compared to the control group.

By how much do protected area systems reduce deforestation? Global efforts to reduce tropical deforestation rely on protected areas, which are sited on the basis of characteristics correlated with deforestation. Using spatial data and matching methods to control for observable sources of bias (and potential spillovers from protected to unprotected lands), Andam, Ferraro, Pfaff, Sanchez-Azofeifa, and Robalino (2008) estimate that less than 10% of protected forest in Costa Rica would have been deforested by 1997 in the absence of protection. Conventional before-after-inside-outside estimates, which fail to control for observable sources of bias, overestimate avoided deforestation by 65% or more.

Do protected areas improve local health and incomes? Most studies are based on ex ante predictions from historical use data and strong assumptions, or ex post analyses that prove only that the poor live near protected areas. In contrast, Wilkie et al. (2006) are tracking health and livelihood outcomes of 1,000 households that traditionally used resources around four new Gabonese national parks and 1,000 households that live outside the influence of the same parks.

How does the U.S. Endangered Species Act affect species recovery? Most studies lack a clear counterfactual. Ferraro, McIntosh, and Ospina (2007) use matching methods to select control groups of species and estimate how species listed and funded under the act would have fared had they not been listed or funded. The analysis suggests that the act improves outcomes for species only when accompanied by substantial species-specific funding but makes outcomes worse when a species is listed under the act with little or no funding.

How does mandatory reporting affect firms' propensity to violate standards? Information disclosure regulations are increasingly common, but their effects on the behavior of regulated firms are unclear. Bennear and Olmstead (2008) evaluate the impact of a 1996 amendment to the U.S. Safe Drinking Water Act that requires community drinking water suppliers to mail information about water quality to their customers. Using a difference-in-differences panel data design and a regression discontinuity design, they estimate that the amendment reduced the number of health and other violations substantially, by about 50%.

These barriers include nonlinear response outcomes, such as thresholds; high natural rate of outcome variability; treatments that comprise multiple interventions; infrequent data sampling, nonexistent baselines, and large measurement error; long time lag between intervention and response; programs with multiple interventions; complex spillover effects, as when deforestation pressures or animals migrate; large spatial scales of ecological processes and environmental interventions, such as landscapes and airsheds; unique treatment units without comparators, such as restricted habitats of endemic species; and small operations budgets (see Hockings et al. in this issue).

Although such barriers are found in all social policy fields, they are particularly pervasive in the field of environmental policy. Thus not only do environmental practitioners and scientists have little familiarity with appropriate designs but their field is one of the most difficult evaluation settings in which to apply such designs. However, many environmental programs are aimed at affecting human behavior in the short run, either as individuals or as collectives in the form of communities, governments, and firms. From this perspective, environmental programs are not radically different from programs in other social policy fields. Thus, although measuring program impact on environmental outcomes may often be difficult because of the barriers noted above, measuring program impacts on the intermediate impact of behavioral changes can be easier. For example, if hunting is threatening a species, and a program designed to reduce hunting is observed to have no effect on hunting, one could reasonably conclude that the program has had no effect on long-term population dynamics of the threatened species (the converse, however, would not necessarily be true).

Experimental and Quasi-Experimental Designs in Environmental Program Evaluation

Experimental and quasi-experimental designs focus on selecting the best representation of the counterfactual. They allow evaluators to collect data in a way that produces sufficient variation in key variables to allow identification and measurement of program impact on relevant outcome indicators.

Experimental Designs. Experiments induce variation by controlling how the data are collected. The most popular way of inducing this variation is through randomization of the program assignment. Probability thus enters the experiment only through random assignment, a process controlled by the experimenter. Randomization is the most popular way of inducing exogenous variation in an experiment because it is easily understood by analysts and practitioners alike. For the same reasons, I focus on randomization, but there are other ways to induce exogenous variation so that program assignment is not correlated with outcomes (Heckman, 2005).

Randomized experiments are most easily and cheaply implemented when the program has one stage and few treatment variations. They are often possible in the context of pilot programs that leave some people, communities, or sites as controls. For example, in programs with more eligible participants than the budget can support, one can randomly choose participants among the relevant population. For programs that cannot randomly restrict access, a random encouragement design might be possible where members of the target population are encouraged at random to participate. In programs that are phased in over time, one can randomly select which participants receive the treatment first, thereby allowing the later participants to serve as controls for the early participants.

New Directions for Evaluation • DOI: 10.1002/ev

Despite the widespread presence of these facilitating conditions in the field of environmental policy, randomized experiments are rare. Published studies are most prevalent among social psychologists that test the effect of conservation messages on individual behaviors, such as littering and energy consumption (see references in Oskamp & Schultz, 2006). Other experiments situate themselves on the boundary of health and the environment, such as the impact of improved wood stoves on indoor air pollution and household health (see Figure 7.1).

In recent years, the number of current and proposed randomized environmental evaluations has increased. These include experiments to test the impact of (1) conservation education messages on individual and collective behavior in the United States (water consumption, voting behavior); (2) payments for environmental services on forest cover and household welfare in Vietnam and Uganda (using randomization at the village level, rather than the individual level); (3) adoption of improved wood stoves on health and economic welfare in India and of compact fluorescent light bulb adoption on energy use in Africa (randomly assign subsidies to purchase lights); and (4) third-party shade-grown coffee certification on environmental and economic outcomes in Latin America.

I do not wish to glorify experimental designs, particularly those that use randomization, whose limitations have been widely debated in the literature (for example, ineffective randomization; randomization biases in which the experimental design itself affects behavior; the inability of unaided randomization to estimate the fraction of a population that benefits from a program). Nevertheless, experimental designs can be particularly helpful in contexts in which there are many plausible biases. Moreover, they can serve as a complement to the quasi-experimental designs discussed in the next section and to nonexperimental designs.

Quasi-Experimental Designs. When true experimental designs are not feasible for political, financial, legal, practical, or ethical reasons, a quasi-experimental design might be possible using available data. If executed with appropriate statistical methods and in full recognition of their limitations, such designs can provide better information about causal impact than nonexperimental designs, especially when quantitative data are available. As in experimental designs, reliability depends on the analyst's ability to specify the counterfactual.

Quasi-experimental designs fall into two categories: (1) designs, such as matching and cross-sectional regressions, which assume treatment assignments are affected only by observable variables for which one can collect data and control in the analysis; and (2) designs that assume treatment assignment takes place on variables that are both observable and unobservable to the analyst. The latter include panel data designs (fixed effects models that control for time-invariant unobservables), as well as "natural experiments," which take advantage of situations in which treatment status is determined by nature, politics, an accident, or some other action beyond the researcher's control (including regression discontinuity; Trochim, 1984; and instrumental variable designs). In some cases, natural experiments only mimic a program but allow one to draw inferences about a hypothetical program's impacts. For example, a recession that lowers pollution emissions may allow one to test the health impacts of a policy that explicitly restricts emissions (Chay & Greenstone, 2003), or widespread forest fires may allow one to estimate health impacts of indoor air pollution programs (Jayachandran, 2008). Quasi-experimental designs are often supplemented by testing the sensitivity of results to potential unobservable confounders or by using tests of known effects to detect the presence of hidden bias (Rosenbaum, 2002).

As in all impact evaluations, the validity of the inference rests on the assumption that assignment to treatment and control groups is not related to other determinants of the outcomes. In category (1) above, treatment is assumed to be unrelated to outcomes, conditional on observable characteristics. In category (2), the independence of treatment and outcomes is asserted through an argument based on knowledge of the program implementation or the known relationship between variables (for example, a variable known to affect who is exposed to a program but uncorrelated with the outcome).

In contrast to the paucity of evaluations using experimental designs, there are dozens of evaluations in the environmental field using quasi-experimental designs (see Figure 7.1 for a few examples). Despite the greater number of examples in the literature, quasi-experimental analyses still make up a small proportion of the environmental evaluation literature.

As with all evaluation designs, one must consider not only their internal validity (i.e., whether one is actually estimating a causal relationship rather than hidden biases) but also their construct validity (whether one is actually measuring the outcome and treatment one reports to be measuring) and external validity (whether the results would be the same for other people, places, or times). These issues, however, are largely context-specific rather than design-specific.

The Future of Environmental Program Impact Evaluations

Counterfactual thinking is important in *any* evaluation seeking to identify program impacts. The best way to promote such thinking is through experimental or quasi-experimental designs that attempt to collect data so that an actual treatment effect would be visibly different from the most plausible hidden biases (Rosenbaum, 2002). Most environmental programs will not be amenable to evaluation as true experiments; nor will they be amenable to sophisticated quasi-experimental designs that require advanced statistical methods, large sample sizes, and rich data sets. Indeed, *most* environmental programs cannot be evaluated with such designs.

Nevertheless, even case study analyses are much more informative when exposed to counterfactual thinking and quasi-experimental designs that collect data so that a treatment effect can be distinguished from hidden biases (Yin, 2003). Most environmental programs should, at a minimum, formulate complex theories of change (causal hypotheses with explicit assumptions); make observations, including at the baseline, on a few important indicators of key theoretical assumptions and outcomes (for example, behavioral changes); consider the likelihood that confounding factors are also affecting outcomes (in other words, carefully consider rival explanations of the observed outcomes); and then make informed judgments about how the program can be changed on the basis of the program's own evidence and evidence from analyses with better internal validity done elsewhere.

Not all environmental programs are amenable to experimental or quasi-experimental designs, but surely *some* of the thousands of environmental programs initiated globally every year are. Although challenges to using these designs exist, their use is no more expensive or complicated than the biological and chemical assessments that are routinely used to develop indicators and to improve understanding of environmental processes. The promise of such designs lies in their ability to complement nonexperimental evaluations and intuition. However, until environmental scientists and practitioners become more aware of these designs and have the incentives and capacity to use them, little progress will be made in building the evidence base for environmental policy.

References

Andam, K., Ferraro, P. J., Pfaff, A., Sanchez-Azofeifa, A., & Robalino, J. (2008). Measuring the effectiveness of protected area networks in reducing deforestation. *Proceedings of the National Academy of Sciences, 105*(41).

Bennear, L. S., & Coglianese, C. (2005). Measuring progress: Program evaluation of environmental policies. *Environment, 47*(2), 22–39.

Bennear, L. S., & Olmstead, S. M. (2008). The impacts of the 'Right to Know': Information disclosure and the violation of drinking water standards. *Journal of Environmental Economics and Management, 56*(2), 117–130.

Chay, K. Y., & Greenstone, M. (2003). The impact of air pollution on infant mortality: Evidence from geographic variation in pollution shocks induced by a recession. *Quarterly Journal of Economics, 188*(3), 1121–1167.

Diaz, E., Smith-Sivertsen, T., Pope, D., Lie, R. T., Diaz, A., McCracken, J., et al. (2007). Eye discomfort, headache and back pain among Mayan Guatemalan women taking part in a randomized stove intervention trial. *Journal of Epidemiology and Community Health, 61*(1), 74–79.

Ferraro, P. J., McIntosh, C., & Ospina, M. (2007). The effectiveness of the U.S. Endangered Species Act: Econometric analysis using matching methods. *Journal of Environmental Economics and Management, 54*(3), 245–261.

Ferraro, P. J., & Pattanayak, S. K. (2006). Money for nothing? A call for empirical evaluation of biodiversity conservation investments. *PLoS Biology, 4*(4), 482–488.

Frondel, M., & Schmidt, C. M. (2005). Evaluating environmental programs: The perspective of modern evaluation research. *Ecological Economics, 55*(4), 515–526.

Greenstone, M., & Gayer, T. (2007). *Quasi-experimental and experimental approaches to environmental economics.* http://papers.ssrn.com/sol3/papers.cfm?abstract_id=1001330

Heckman, J. J. (2005). Rejoinder: Response to Sobel. *Sociological Methodology, 35*(1), 135–162.

IPCC. (2007). *Climate change 2007: Mitigation of climate change. Contribution of Working Group III to the Fourth Assessment Report of the Intergovernmental Panel on Climate Change.* Cambridge: Cambridge University Press.

Jayachandran, S. (2008). *Air quality and early life mortality: Evidence from Indonesia's wildfires.* http://www.stanford.edu/~jayachan/indo_fires.pdf

Millennium Ecosystem Assessment (MA). (2005). *Ecosystems and human well-being: Policy responses.* Washington, DC: Island Press.

Mulville-Friel, D., & Anderson, D. (1996, August). Measuring effectiveness. *Florida Water Resources Journal,* 18–20.

Oskamp, S., & Schultz, P. W. (2006). Using psychological science to achieve ecological sustainability. In S. I. Donaldson, D. E. Berger, & K. Pezdek (Eds.), *Applied psychology: New frontiers and rewarding careers* (pp. 81–106). New York: Routledge Press.

Pullin, A. S., & Knight, T. M. (2001). Effectiveness in conservation practice: Pointers from medicine and public health. *Conservation Biology, 15*(1), 50–54.

Rosenbaum, P. (2002). *Observational studies.* New York: Springer-Verlag.

Saterson, K. A., Christensen, N. L., Jackson, R. B., Kramer, R. A., Pimm, S. L., Smith, M. D., & Wiener, J. B. (2004). Effectiveness in conservation practice: Pointers from medicine and public health. *Conservation Biology, 18,* 597–599.

Stem, C., Margoluis, R., Salfasky, N., & Brown, M. (2005). Monitoring and evaluation in conservation: A review of trends and approaches. *Conservation Biology, 19*(2), 295–309.

Sutherland, W. J., Pullin, A. S., Dolman, P. M., & Knight, T. M. (2004). The need for evidence-based conservation. *Trends in Ecology and Evolution, 19*(6), 305–308.

Trochim, W. (1984). *Research design for program evaluation: The regression-discontinuity approach.* Beverly Hills, CA: Sage.

Wilkie, D., Morelli, G., Demmer, J., Starkey, M., Telfer, P., & Steil, M. (2006). Parks and people: Assessing the human welfare effects of establishing protected areas for biodiversity conservation. *Conservation Biology, 20*(1), 247–249.

Yin, R. K. (2003). *Case study research: design and methods.* Thousand Oaks, CA: Sage.

PAUL J. FERRARO is an associate professor of economics in the Andrew Young School of Policy Studies at Georgia State University.

Margoluis, R., Stem, C., Salafsky, N., & Brown, M. (2009). Design alternatives for evaluating the impact of conservation projects. In M. Birnbaum & P. Mickwitz (Eds.), *Environmental program and policy evaluation: Addressing methodological challenges. New Directions for Evaluation, 122,* 85–96.

8

Design Alternatives for Evaluating the Impact of Conservation Projects

Richard Margoluis, Caroline Stem, Nick Salafsky, Marcia Brown

Abstract

Historically, examples of project evaluation in conservation were rare. In recent years, however, conservation professionals have begun to recognize the importance of evaluation both for accountability and for improving project interventions. Even with this growing interest in evaluation, the conservation community has paid little attention to evaluation design. Recent literature includes some discussion of design, but it has focused primarily on experimental and quasi-experimental design and the use of counterfactuals. Real-life conservation projects, however, operate in complex and dynamic contexts and under conditions of limited resources, which limit the feasibility of counterfactual or experimental designs. There is, in fact, a range of design options to evaluate conservation interventions. The conservation community must educate itself about these options, and how different designs produce different results. This chapter discusses evaluation design alternatives in light of the unique challenges that influence evaluation design selection in conservation. © Wiley Periodicals, Inc.

The conservation profession has matured to the point at which it must demonstrate positive results and wise use of conservation dollars. No longer is the adage "trust us; we are doing good work" sufficient to satisfy supporters and society at large. Given both the general calls for accountability and the stakes involved in conserving resources for future generations, we can ill afford to be inefficient in selecting interventions; we must learn and document what works and does not work in order to improve conservation decisions.

Despite all the thinking and experience in program evaluation over the past decades, the conservation community has not successfully applied this knowledge to conservation evaluation. Many researchers and practitioners recognize the utility of systematic evaluation, yet they rarely apply it. In fact, there is scant evidence of the use of the range of evaluation approaches regularly applied in fields such as public health, community development, and education (Stem, Margoluis, Salafsky, & Brown, 2005).

Although there has been some recent discussion of evaluation design in the conservation literature, much of it has centered on the role of experimental and quasi-experimental design and use of counterfactuals (Ferraro & Pattanayak, 2006; and Ferraro, this issue). But typically, real-life conservation projects operate in complex and dynamic contexts and under conditions of limited resources. In these real-world situations, it is often not feasible to use counterfactual or experimental designs (Donaldson & Christie, 2005; Mark & Henry, 2006; Bamberger, Rugh, & Mabry, 2006).

There is, in fact, a range of options to evaluate conservation interventions. Conservation evaluators and managers, however, are largely unaware of these options and lack guidance on how to determine which to use. Although there is no one right way to do an evaluation, there are some general considerations for choosing a design: (1) purpose of the evaluation, (2) program structure and circumstances, (3) resources available for the evaluation, and (4) capacity of those doing the evaluation (Rossi, Freeman, & Lipsey, 1999). Collectively, they influence the extent to which evaluators can use control or comparison groups and the amount, type, and quality of data they can collect. Reality dictates that the type of approach chosen must involve trade-offs on issues such as precision, cost, and buy-in. As such, not all evaluations need or should strive to produce results that establish absolute causality, maximize external validity, and rule out all other explanations (Donaldson & Christie, 2005; Mark & Henry, 2006). The main question evaluators must resolve is whether they have to show that all signs point to an intervention working or whether they need to produce irrefutable scientific proof that the intervention works.

This paper lays out designs available for evaluating conservation actions. It focuses on evaluation for management effectiveness (Stem et al., 2005) and not on status assessment, or methods and tools that are somewhat independent of design and thus can be applied across a range of evaluation designs (Margoluis & Salafsky, 1998). Finally, this chapter attempts to describe when various evaluation designs should be applied and how approaches may be combined.

Design Options for Conservation Evaluations

Trochim (2006) defines research design as "the glue that holds the research project together. A design is used to structure the research, to show how . . . the samples or groups, measures, treatments or programs, and methods of assignment work together to try to address the central research questions." This definition easily applies to evaluation design as well. Drawing on this definition, we identify these elements of evaluation design: sampling methods, use (or not) of controls and comparisons, timing of interventions, and timing of observation(s).

As in other fields, conservation evaluation may be based on quantitative or qualitative data (Figure 8.1). Quantitative evaluation can be divided into three broad categories: experimental, quasi-experimental, and nonexperimental (Rossi et al., 1999). Qualitative evaluation relies heavily on purposefully sampling a relatively small number of cases or key informants and rarely uses counterfactuals (Patton, 2002). Qualitative sampling methods are not completely distinct from quantitative evaluation designs in that some qualitative sampling methods can be applied to quasi-experimental and nonexperimental designs (e.g., criterion sampling or stratified purposeful sampling). Nevertheless, we include them in this discussion because they are all evaluation approaches available to conservation practitioners.

Figure 8.1 also discusses internal and external validity, which are key issues in evaluation design. We do not discuss construct validity here because it is largely independent of evaluation design and therefore less relevant to this chapter.

Historically, most conservation evaluations have been purely descriptive in nature, relying heavily on subjective analysis. At best, these evaluations have tended to be qualitative, with little or no deliberate attention to evaluation design. Almost always, they are ex post in nature. When conservation evaluations do attempt to infer causality, the most commonly used designs are nonexperimental (i.e., the only sample measured is the one exposed to the conservation intervention).

In this chapter, we briefly discuss some key design options and provide examples of how these options might be best used in conservation. We do not emphasize experimental design here because we believe it is not a particularly cost-beneficial option for real-world conservation projects that wish to conduct management effectiveness evaluation.

Quantitative Designs. Quantitative evaluation design includes experimental, quasi-experimental, and nonexperimental designs. These designs allow population-based analysis of an intervention's impact. In particular, units are identified and sampled so as to allow inference of a population. If a sample has been selected without bias, statistical generalizations can be

Figure 8.1. Types of Evaluation Design

Quantitative Design

1. **Experimental:** random assignment of subjects to treated (experimental) and untreated (control) groups
   Advantages: approximates counterfactual condition; strong evidence for causality
   Limitations: expensive; often not practical; ethical issues; high expertise

   Validity:
   Internal: high; random assignments; strongest design for internal validity
   External: low; artificial setting limits ability to generalize to other settings

   Example: *Randomized pre and post:* researcher randomly assigns items into control and experimental groups. Measurements taken before and after intervention

2. **Quasi-experimental:** similar to experimental but lacks random assignment
   Advantages: easier to establish than true experimental designs; fairly strong evidence for causality
   Limitations: moderately expensive to expensive

   Validity:
   Internal: moderate; inability to randomly assign controls, lack of control over variables
   External: moderate; "natural experiments" allow some generalization

   Examples:
   A. *Matched controls:* intervention group matched with controls selected by researcher
   B. *Regression-discontinuity:* pretest/posttest design in which participants are assigned to program or comparison groups on the basis of a cutoff score on a preprogram measure
   C. *Statistically equated controls:* exposed and unexposed groups or items compared by means of statistical controls
   D. *Generic controls:* exposed group or items compared with outcome measures available on general population

3. **Nonexperimental:** draws inferences about the effect of a treatment on subjects, where assignment of subjects into a treated versus control group is outside the researcher's control
   Advantages: least expensive quantitative design; easier to implement
   Limitations: observe state of world without manipulating it, so less power to detect causal relationships

   Validity:
   Internal: low; no randomization, no controls
   External: moderate; natural settings make generalizability stronger

   Examples:
   A. *Pretest/posttest:* subjects measured before and after intervention

B. *Time series:* large aggregates taken on large population and compared before and after intervention

C. *Cross-sectional studies for nonuniform programs:* subjects differentially exposed to intervention compared with statistical controls

Qualitative Design

4. **Qualitative sampling options:** qualitative evaluation design options focus almost exclusively on the sampling framework and not statistical power or how exposed and nonexposed cases are compared. Individual cases are weighted more heavily because the evaluator is not looking for population-based trends.

   Advantages: generally, less expensive than experimental and quasi-experimental designs; rich data and anecdotes

   Limitations: analysis more difficult; subjective interpretations

   Validity:

   Internal: low; no randomization, no controls; researcher interpretation, interviewee perception, recall accuracy

   External: low; if cases are carefully selected and analyzed over extended period of time, can be moderate

   Examples (see Patton, 2002, for more):

   A. *Stratified purposeful sampling:* stratifying samples within samples by selecting particular cases that vary according to a key dimension, thus facilitating comparison

   B. *Extreme or deviant case sampling:* learning from highly unusual manifestations of issue of interest (e.g., outstanding successes and notable failures, top of the class or dropouts)

   C. *Theory-based or operational construct sampling:* sampling subjects on basis of their potential manifestation of a theoretical construct so as to elaborate and examine the construct

---

made from the sample to the population. Quantitative design is most useful to isolate the effects of specific variables of interest.

Quasi-Experimental Designs. Quasi-experimental designs are most appropriate when conservation evaluators want to test the efficacy of a specific conservation tool, cannot take a true experimental approach, and need to have relatively high confidence that the observed effect of the intervention is real. These designs require good knowledge of sampling, instrument and protocol design, and statistics.

One quasi-experimental design option that is virtually nonexistent in conservation but that has enormous potential is matched control/comparison groups. Like other quasi-experimental approaches, the matched controls/comparison group design mimics experimental design, but it lacks random assignment of exposed and comparison groups. Those units that are exposed to a conservation intervention are "matched" with

New Directions for Evaluation • DOI: 10.1002/ev

units that are not exposed. Matching occurs on key variables and controls for potential differences between the two groups, thus isolating the effects of the intervention.

Margoluis et al. (2001) used a matched control/comparison design to determine the utility of sustainable agriculture as a conservation tool. Researchers interviewed farmers who participated in a sustainable agriculture program. Each sustainable agriculture farmer ("user") family was matched to a farmer family that did not use sustainable agriculture ("nonuser") techniques. Matched variables included access to goods and services, socioeconomic status, and distance to available agricultural lands. Data collection occurred in two similar biosphere sites in Mexico and Guatemala. Evaluation results demonstrated that users in Mexico planted less area with corn and beans than nonusers, thus reducing the deforestation rates. Conversely, in Guatemala users planted more area with corn and beans than nonusers did, thus increasing the deforestation rate. This design permitted evaluators to isolate the effects of a specific tool and assess the difference between two seemingly similar sites. The three independent variables that predicted the observed differences between Mexico and Guatemala were land tenure status, government land use rights policy, and proximity to protected areas.

Nonexperimental Designs. Nonexperimental designs are most appropriate when conservation evaluators want to determine whether there is a relationship between an intervention and an impact, but they do not have the resources to use an experimental or quasi-experimental design, or they do not have access to an adequate control or comparison group. Although results from evaluations employing these designs can be quite useful for management decisions, the designs themselves are generally less rigorous and thus may not require the same level of technical and statistical expertise that quasi-experimental and experimental designs require.

One of the most basic nonexperimental designs involves measuring exposed units before and after an intervention (pretest, posttest, and time series designs). Despite its simplicity and power to infer causality, it is rarely used in conservation. Nevertheless, it is well suited for some common interventions, such as environmental education or media campaigns where one wants to see a change in knowledge, attitudes, or behavior.

A specific example can be found in Powers (2004), where the author evaluated a forestry field visit for second grade students using a pretest-posttest design to assess changes in attitudes and knowledge prior to and following the field experiences. One of the most revealing findings was that socioeconomic variables showed stronger associations with attitude and knowledge changes than did field visit length. The greatest change in knowledge and attitudes was seen in students who participated in the program for only one day but came from communities with less access to forestry settings. Similar environmental education studies using a time-series design are Brossard, Lewenstein, and Bonney (2005) and DiEnno and Hilton (2005).

Qualitative Design Options. Qualitative evaluation designs permit in-depth analysis of a particular subject. They commonly focus on knowledge, perceptions, attitudes, and behavior. Typically, qualitative designs are variations of case-study approaches in which key individuals are interviewed as special cases that can elucidate a specific subject. Sampling, therefore, is not population-based and thus does not lend itself to statistical analysis. Moreover, qualitative design rarely involves the use of control or comparison groups. Even so, well-designed case studies can be used for theory development, hypothesis testing, and generalization beyond the individual case (Flyvbjerg 2006). Some common general approaches to qualitative design are participatory appraisal, fourth generation evaluation, and utilization-focused evaluation (Chambers, 1997; Guba & Lincoln, 1989; Patton, 1997).

Qualitative designs include several potential sampling strategies (Patton, 2002), sampling being a main element of an evaluation design. A common qualitative sampling strategy in other fields though rarely used in conservation, is stratified purposeful sampling. Stratified sampling divides a population into relatively discrete groups based on key variables. Purposeful sampling involves selecting a relatively small group of units within each stratum to control for potentially important differences among them.

A hypothetical example of this design involves a conservation and development project to increase household income. Project managers hope to reduce overharvesting of a bamboo species that is an important food for key animal species. The managers believe that providing an alternative to bamboo collection that yields greater financial return on less invested labor will lead community members to harvest less. The evaluators use a wealth ranking tool to analyze community wealth distribution and identify four discrete economic classes or "strata." For each stratum, the evaluators purposefully identify, select, and interview ten heads-of-household to determine if the project had any influence on their behavior and if this outcome varied across the wealth categories.

This design cannot generate statistical evidence of the intervention's impact, but it can provide insightful evidence of the difference between groups, and why these differences occur. Results could also inform future quantitative evaluation activities, such as a subsequent household survey, or they could help explain findings from an initial quantitative survey.

Discussion

The design options presented here hold much promise for conservation evaluation. Quasi-experimental designs generally yield the greatest internal validity while quasi- and nonexperimental designs offer greater external validity and are more precise than qualitative approaches. Qualitative approaches, however, are generally more adaptable and produce more in-depth, revealing information regarding *why* an intervention has worked or not. As such,

NEW DIRECTIONS FOR EVALUATION • DOI: 10.1002/ev

depending on the question asked, an evaluator may choose a qualitative or quantitative design.

What Are Unique Challenges to Evaluation in Conservation?. The conservation community needs to educate itself about evaluation design options and how different designs produce different results. Nevertheless, there are unique challenges that influence evaluation design selection in conservation. To fully tap into the power of different evaluation designs, the conservation community must address these challenges, and in many ways change how it operates. Among these challenges:

- *The units acted on are often not the units conservation projects want to ultimately influence.* A public health project might provide immunizations to children in a community. The intervention is on children, and the ultimate impact is measured in terms of the children's health. In contrast, conservation projects are often designed to influence individuals, governments, or societies, but their impact is measured in terms of species and ecosystem health. Not surprisingly, extrapolating from an intervention aimed at humans to an impact on species or ecosystems is complex and challenging.
- *Conservation projects usually take place in large, complex settings.* Whether a large site such as the Amazon Basin or a global theme such as climate change, conservation initiatives work in complex, dynamic, and often unpredictable circumstances.
- *Relevant secondary data are rarely available.* Conservation project evaluation requires biological and biophysical data for the dependent variables. Although many conservation researchers and organizations collect this type of data, there is often little coordination between their agendas and those of project teams. Consequently, if secondary data do exist for a project site, they are often not the right data or at the right scale to answer management questions. Conservation organizations therefore must collect primary data for evaluation purposes. This is often costly and difficult to do.
- *Evaluation is rarely incorporated into program design.* Most conservation evaluations are an afterthought with no attention to evaluation requirements at a program's inception. As a result, no baseline data are collected, and little or no data are collected throughout the project's life.
- *Conservation planning and evaluation require knowledge of and expertise in social and biological sciences.* Recently, the conservation community has been somewhat divided into "biologist" and "social scientist" camps and has done little to integrate social and biological data. This integration is crucial because ultimate impact is measured in terms of species and ecosystem health while intermediate outcomes are typically measured in terms of human knowledge, attitudes, and behavior.
- *Conceptual linkages among interventions, outcomes, and impacts are relatively unknown.* Because conservation is a relatively new field, many of the conceptual underpinnings that delineate associations and potential causality among interventions, outcomes, and impacts are untested and

unknown. Designing conservation evaluations at the outset, therefore, is especially challenging because data requirements are unclear and expected results are unpredictable.

- The *time lag between intervention and impact is often very long*. Although not exclusive to conservation, it is especially problematic in this field. Because of life cycles and natural fluctuations in species and ecosystems that occur over many decades, changes attributable to a particular intervention are difficult to establish.
- *Urgency drives program planning more than evidence of success does*. The conservation field is one driven by perceived urgency to act; thus there has historically been little will to "divert" precious program dollars to evaluation activities. Consequently, the field has not been too systematic in learning about which interventions work best under which conditions.

What Can the Conservation Field Do to Address These Challenges? To overcome these challenges and be better prepared to choose the right design, we suggest a number of evaluation-related principles.

Build Appropriate Evaluation Design Into Program Design. Conservation practitioners and evaluators must consider expected outcomes at the outset—not only at the end—of a project, and they must collect baseline data. They must also understand the conditions under which specific evaluation designs are appropriate. In particular, we call for an end to the false dichotomy that pits the use of counterfactuals against all other forms of evaluation. The question is not, "Which is the best evaluation design in conservation?" Instead, it should be, "What is the best evaluation design option available to conservation managers for their circumstances?"

Ensure an Adequate Theory of Change. Most conservationists erroneously believe that by measuring only the dependent variable (e.g., species and ecosystems), one can tell if conservation interventions have been successful. In fact, to reach this conclusion one must measure incremental change at various points along a theory of change, from the intervention to intermediate outcomes to ultimate impacts (Foundations of Success, 2007). What interventions led to knowledge change? What knowledge change led to attitude change? What attitude change led to behavior change? What behavior change led to a mitigation of threats? Which threat mitigation led to species or ecosystem improvement? These "incremental evaluations" help evaluators break down complexity, understand system components, and reconstruct an understanding of the conditions within which interventions operate. They also foster incremental learning and help develop a body of evidence—a plausible case for association, causality, and ultimately conservation impact.

Partner With Organizations That Have the Expertise to Collect Social Data. Until the conservation community builds its internal capacity to effectively measure the human dimensions of conservation, it should seek partners in relevant fields to identify appropriate indicators, collect and analyze data, and link changes in human dimensions to changes in biological dimensions.

NEW DIRECTIONS FOR EVALUATION • DOI: 10.1002/ev

Bridge Biologist-Social Scientist and Practitioner-Researcher Gaps. Conservation organizations should add to their staff individuals with training and experience in bridging the social and biological divides who are capable of playing both programmatic and evaluative roles. These individuals can help create a robust subfield of operations research (as in public health) that accelerates learning and optimizes effectiveness. Likewise, conservation organizations should work closely with scientists to coordinate research agendas to help answer important management questions.

Do Not Sacrifice What Is Important for What Is Urgent. If the conservation community is to make concrete advances in understanding which tools and strategies work best under which conditions, it must stop, look, listen, analyze, and learn; that is, it must vastly improve its ability to evaluate actions. To do this, it should invest more heavily in its capacity to design and implement effective evaluations.

How Can Design Alternatives Help the Conservation Community Overcome These Challenges? The evaluation design option that is most appropriate to a given conservation situation depends on the purpose of the

Table 8.1. Conservation Evaluation Scenarios and Potential Designs

Scenario	Example of Appropriate Design or Approach
A large conservation organization wishes to gauge the effectiveness of its policy reform campaign to change greenhouse gas emission laws.	Qualitative purposeful sampling in which members of Congress are interviewed
A foundation wants to see how effective its partner capacity building program is.	Nonexperimental, time series in which participants are interviewed three times before and three times after participating in a training program
A government agency with limited evaluation capacity wants to know whether an increase in park fees has improved park conservation.	Mixed method approach: 1. Review of secondary data (accounting books) 2. Qualitative purposeful sampling in which park rangers are interviewed to determine their perceptions regarding changes in animal populations
A regional marine conservation organization wants to gauge the impact of its "best management practices" program for fishermen.	Quasi-experimental matching in which fishermen who use new technologies are compared to those who do not
A national conservation organization wishes to measure the success of its media campaign to buy certified wood.	Nonexperimental, pretest/posttest with a large sample in which consumers nationwide are interviewed on exiting a national home improvement store
A small conservation organization with limited resources wants to know if its income generation project is working.	Qualitative purposeful sampling in which four age classes of women participating in the project are compared

evaluation, program structure and circumstances, resources available, and the capacity of those doing the evaluation (Rossi et al., 1999). One tactic to draw on the merits of both qualitative and quantitative design is to use a mixed-method approach. Mixed methods offer a variety of benefits (Patton, 2002; Bamberger et al., 2006; Greene, Kreider, & Mayer, 2005) to strengthen conservation evaluations. The examples in Table 8.1 illustrate a range of potential options for how conservation evaluators could use different evaluation designs and approaches under different conditions.

Conclusions

Evaluation is not a one-size-fits-all endeavor. The "best" evaluation design for a project will vary widely by factors including available time and funding, existing expertise, and level of precision needed. Trade-offs are inevitable. Does one invest large sums of money over a long time to establish causality with certainty? Or does one seize an opportunity to learn quickly and adapt in a dynamic, changing world? Less rigorous evaluation designs mean there will be situations where evaluators and practitioners miss causal links and make the wrong decision. Good, continuous, systematic monitoring, however, is crucial because it allows practitioners to tweak their actions as they implement, catching poor decisions early. Unfortunately, this type of monitoring and adapting is all too rare in conservation.

We have briefly described the range of options available to evaluate conservation project effectiveness and some design considerations that are somewhat unique to conservation. We also have attempted to show how they can be used effectively by themselves or in combination for robust evaluation findings.

Evaluation in conservation is not only about measuring effectiveness. It is also about engaging the conservation community. If we disassociate evaluation from practice, we will lose the practitioners and as a result their commitment to using evaluation results. To ensure evaluation leads to management decisions, conservation managers must engage in choosing the right evaluation design. More generally, the conservation community needs to discuss which evaluation designs work for its practitioners and under what circumstances they are most appropriate. With this chapter, we hope to take an initial step in that direction.

References

Bamberger, M., Rugh, J., & Mabry, L. (2006). *Real world evaluation: Working under budget, time, data and political constraints.* Thousand Oaks, CA: Sage.

Brossard, D., Lewenstein, B., & Bonney, R. (2005). Scientific knowledge and attitude change: The impact of a citizen science project. *International Journal of Science Education, 27*(9), 1099–1121.

Chambers, R. (1997). *Whose reality counts? Putting the first last.* London: Intermediate Technology.

DiEnno, C. M., & Hilton, S. C. (2005). High school students' knowledge, attitudes, and levels of enjoyment of an environmental education unit on nonnative plants. *Journal of Environmental Education, 37*(1), 13–25.

Donaldson, S. I., & Christie, C. A. (2005). The 2004 Claremont Debate: Lipsey vs. Scriven—Determining causality in program evaluation and applied research: Should experimental evidence be the gold standard? *Journal of Multidisciplinary Evaluation, 3,* 60–77.

Ferraro, P. J., & Pattanayak, S. K. (2006). Money for nothing? A call for empirical evaluation of biodiversity conservation investments. *PLoS Biology, 4*(4), 105.

Flyvbjerg, B. (2006). Five misunderstandings about case-study research. *Qualitative Inquiry, 2*(2), 219–245.

Foundations of Success. (2007). *Using results chains to improve strategy effectiveness.* Bethesda, MD: Author.

Greene, J. C., Kreider, H., & Mayer, E. (2005). Combining qualitative and quantitative methods in social inquiry. In B. Somekh & C. Lewin (Eds.), *Research methods in the social sciences* (pp. 274–281). London: Sage.

Guba, E. G., & Lincoln, Y. S. (1989). *Fourth generation evaluation.* Newbury Park, CA: Sage.

Margoluis, R., Russell, V., Gonzalez, M., Rojas, O., Magdaleno, J., Madrid, G., et al. (2001). *Maximum yield? Sustainable agriculture as a tool for conservation.* Washington, DC: Biodiversity Support Program.

Margoluis, R., & Salafsky, N. (1998). *Measures of success: Designing, managing, and monitoring conservation and development projects.* Washington, DC: Island Press.

Mark, M., & Henry, G. (2006). Methods for policy-making and knowledge development evaluations. In I. Shaw, J. Greene, & M. Mark (Eds.), *Handbook of evaluation: Policies, programs and practices* (pp. 317–339). Thousand Oaks, CA: Sage.

Mark, M. M., Henry, G. T., & Julnes, G. (2000). *Evaluation: An integrated framework for understanding, guiding, and improving policies and programs.* San Francisco: Jossey-Bass.

Patton, M. Q. (1997). *Utilization-focused evaluation: The new century text* (3rd ed.). Thousand Oaks, CA: Sage.

Patton, M. Q. (2002). *Qualitative evaluation and research methods* (3rd ed.). Thousand Oaks, CA: Sage.

Powers, A. L. (2004). Evaluation of one- and two-day forestry field programs for elementary school children. *Applied Environmental Education and Communication, 3*(1), 39–46.

Rossi, P. H., Freeman, H. E., & Lipsey, M. W. (1999). *Evaluation: A systematic approach* (6th ed.). Thousand Oaks, CA: Sage.

Stem, C., Margoluis, R., Salafsky, N., & Brown, M. (2005). Monitoring and evaluation in conservation: A review of trends and approaches. *Conservation Biology, 19*(2), 295–309.

Trochim, W. M. (2006). *The research methods knowledge base* (2nd ed.). Retrieved version current as of October 20, 2006, from http://www.socialresearchmethods.net/kb/

RICHARD MARGOLUIS, CAROLINE STEM, NICK SALAFSKY, *and* MARCIA BROWN *are affiliated with Foundations of Success (FOS) in Bethesda, Maryland.*

Preskill, H. (2009). Reflections on the dilemmas of conducting environmental evaluations.
In M. Birnbaum & P. Mickwitz (Eds.), *Environmental program and policy evaluation:
Addressing methodological challenges. New Directions for Evaluation, 122*, 97–103.

9

Reflections on the Dilemmas of Conducting Environmental Evaluations

Hallie Preskill

Abstract

*The chapters in this volume set a rich context for understanding the challenges
that environmental evaluators face in their everyday work. In particular, the
authors highlight the need for responsive, contextual, flexible, adaptive, multidisciplinary, and mixed-methods evaluation approaches. In this chapter, I rein-
force their call and further suggest that they (1) increase their attention to
developing logic models based on their theories of change, (2) continue exploring the use of complexity theory to ground their evaluations, and (3) consider
reframing some evaluations to being strength- and asset-based, where vibrancy,
resiliency, and rebirth can be studied. Finally, in response to the authors' concern for their own development, I comment on the possibilities for evaluation
capacity building and the formation of networks and communities of practice.
© Wiley Periodicals, Inc.*

> Humankind has not woven the web of life. We are but one thread within it.
> Whatever we do to the web, we do to ourselves. All things are bound together.
> All things connect.
>
> —Chief Seattle, 1855

NEW DIRECTIONS FOR EVALUATION, no. 122, Summer 2009 © Wiley Periodicals, Inc., and the American Evaluation
Association. Published online in Wiley InterScience (www.interscience.wiley.com) • DOI: 10.1002/ev.299

When I was asked to write this chapter, my first reaction was to decline. Though I have been designing and conducting evaluations, teaching evaluation, and researching and writing about evaluation for more than 20 years, my practice fields have not intersected much with environmental program evaluation. Nonetheless, I ultimately agreed to participate in this important issue of *New Directions for Evaluation* because I am, like everyone else, merely a visitor to this beautiful and wondrous place we call Earth. Put another way, we shouldn't "blow it—good planets are hard to find" (quoted in *Time,* author and date unknown).

The chapters raise several critical issues and questions about what constitutes meaningful and useful evaluation within dynamic, fluid, and unpredictable social and ecological systems. The authors' questions about how to design and implement evaluations that have varied time horizons, several kinds of stakeholders, and challenges to collecting credible and relevant data are not unique to those studying environmental programs, initiatives, and policies. Certainly those working in the mental health, substance abuse prevention, HIV/AIDs, housing, and education fields, to name a few, are also presented with similar difficulties in studying program effects and impacts. Unfortunately, there is no simple answer to such complex dilemmas; however, what I hope to do in this chapter is bring an outsider's perspective to these issues and offer some humble suggestions for further consideration.

Designing and Implementing Evaluations in Complex Environments

Nearly all of the authors in this issue described their approaches to evaluating various aspects of the environment. Yet I found it curious and rather surprising that few discussed the role of *focusing the evaluation.* By focusing, I mean the first phase of the evaluation process, where we convene a group of stakeholders to (1) develop a program logic model and discuss the program's theory of change or action; (2) determine the evaluation's purpose; (3) identify the primary, secondary, and tertiary stakeholders; and (4) develop key evaluation questions that will focus and guide the evaluation. Although Hildén (Chapter 1) discusses the use of intervention theories; Margoluis, Stem, and two colleagues at FOS (Chapter 8) call attention to the need to explore "conceptual linkages among interventions, outcomes, and impacts"; and Ferraro (Chapter 7) articulates the challenges of developing a program's theory of change, I was a bit surprised that there was so little discussion about the usefulness or use of program logic models. There is no question that logic models have serious limitations in their ability to describe certain kinds of longitudinal impacts and outcomes, and their linearity poses some contradictions to the complexity that exists in ecosystems; nonetheless, they constitute a means for groups of people to articulate an initiative's underlying assumptions, as well as the resources, activities, and expected short-term outputs and outcomes (see Frechtling, 2007; University of Wisconsin

Cooperative Extension, http://www.uwex.edu/ces/pdande/evaluation/pdf/
lmguidecomplete.pdf, retrieved Oct. 20, 2008). At the very least, a logic
model can clarify and make explicit stakeholders' understandings and
expectations; these conversations can be opportunities to detect errors in
thinking or practice before further designing the evaluation. Focusing the
evaluation can also ensure that the evaluation's design and methods are
appropriate and feasible for answering the key evaluation questions. Whether
the desire is to ensure the credibility or relevance of data (Bruyninckx,
Chapter 3; Pullin & Knight, Chapter 6) or use nested approaches (Kennedy,
Balasubramanian, & Crosse, Chapter 4), decisions should be made that take
into account the program's context, goals, and how the results will be used
(by whom and for what kind of decision and action). Though several of the
authors commented on the fact that most evaluations have various levels of
stakeholders who all have their own goals for an evaluation, it seems that
we could do more to involve key stakeholders in a dialogue and decisions
about the purpose of the evaluation and the questions the evaluation will
seek to answer.

The majority of chapters focused on the challenges associated with
choosing an evaluation's design and methods. Those in the evaluation field
have long debated the merits of one design over another (e.g., quantitative
vs. qualitative, RCTs vs. qualitative case studies), but I believe it is safe to
say that most evaluators today support methodological diversity and pluralism. Although the allure and promise of RCTs (randomized control trials) has led to an increased requirement for quantifiable outcomes in the last
several years, many evaluators and funders are finding that studies of this
kind are insufficient for addressing the evaluation's questions; are not appropriate for the particular cultural, organizational, or community context; or
are not yielding the "truth" of what is happening (e.g., Kramer, Graves,
Hirschhorn, & Fiske, 2007; Snibbe, 2006; Woodwell, 2005). Echoing this
sentiment, and lamenting the length of time if often takes to find a program's
impact, Hildén (Chapter 1) writes, "evaluations can therefore seldom produce 'the truth.'" In response to this predicament, he calls for adaptive evaluations that are recursive and repeated during a policy cycle in the hope of
revisiting findings.

Concerned with "black box" designs, Mickwitz and Birnbaum (Editors'
Notes) argue that such designs simply cannot "focus on changing human
behavior while working synergistically with practitioners who are focused
on direct changes to environmental conditions." To ensure that these conditions are considered in the evaluation, the authors in this issue suggest
using an interdisciplinary approach (Bruyninckx, Chapter 3), identifying
and measuring contextual factors (Pullin & Knight, Chapter 6), and inte-
grating quantitative and qualitative data and methods (Hockings, Stolton,
Dudley, & James, Chapter 5; Pullin & Knight, Chapter 6). I strongly believe
that these authors are quite right to call for responsive, contextual, flexible,
adaptive, multidisciplinary, and mixed-methods approaches to evaluation.

Every chapter in this issue also highlights with great clarity the challenge of evaluating dynamic systems that exert influence inside the system while at the same time being affected unpredictably by variables outside the system. I would think that at times an environmental evaluator doesn't know where to focus his or her gaze; in a moment, the setting has changed and a new variable has emerged, or what seemed like an impact has all but disappeared. Clearly, this work is not for the faint of heart. Nor is it for those who need predictability and who struggle with ambiguity! I sense that conducting environmental program evaluations can feel overwhelming at times: Where do I start, where do I look, how do I measure something that is so evolving, fleeting, or that will take so long to see a result? Perhaps the best we can do is to view environmental evaluations as proxies, or approximations of what is happening as a result of any intervention, program, or policy.

Furthermore, instead of operating from a reductionist, linear approach to evaluation where we try to predict and control the future, we might instead consider how complexity theory could inform environmental evaluations. As Eoyang (2006) suggests, "The future is unpredictable because the dynamical interaction of the forces at each point cannot be known in advance" (p. 127). Such evaluations would not only be adaptable and emergent in their evaluation approaches (shifting gears when the environment changes) but would focus on the richness of the context by "*revealing, exploring,* and *challenging* boundary judgments associated with a situation of interest" (Imam, LaGoy, & Williams, 2007, p. 9; emphasis in original). Acknowledgment and support for this approach comes from Margoluis, Stem, and colleagues, who write in Chapter 8, "real-life conservation projects operate in complex and dynamic contexts and under conditions of limited resources." Complexity theory suggests that instead of breaking things apart and studying them, we should look "at the complicated and surprising things which can emerge from the interaction of a collection of objects which themselves may be rather simple" (Johnson, 2007, p. 17). For evaluators, this means being attuned to small changes, interactions among variables (quantitative and qualitative), and looking for patterns in the seemingly disordered data. It also means articulating concretely and explicitly that environmental evaluations are about values and that stakeholders must be involved in the design and implementation of an evaluation as well as be identified as the users of the evaluation findings.

The final observation I would like to make in this section concerns the lens or frame we use in attempting to solve environmental problems and their related evaluations. It seems to me that we have been primarily using a deficit-based model of thinking and practice. For example, Gullison and Hardner (Chapter 2) discuss the use of *limiting factors* in evaluating biodiversity conservation projects. The authors explain that they are using the term to "refer to those factors that present the greatest threat to a biodiversity conservation project." They suggest that this method will help evaluators in "assessing whether current conditions are likely to prevent grantees from achieving their long-term objectives" (from the abstract of Chapter 2). I understand what these authors are saying, but I can't help wondering if this deductive and problem-focused approach might not actually limit our creativity, innovation, and understanding of the process and impact of environmental programs and their evaluations. Could the word *limit* be a self-fulfilling prophecy? For example, what would we learn if instead of looking at "limiting factors," or focusing on what isn't working, we looked for places in the system (or program) that were flourishing, where there was vitality and vibrancy, where there was resiliency, and where new energy was being created? This is not to say that we turn away from addressing problems; rather, by focusing on the strengths in the system, the evaluation questions would shift to identifying ways of increasing and building on what is working. To this point, it would be most interesting to explore how positive psychology concepts, and in particular Appreciative Inquiry, could inform environmental evaluations (see Preskill & Catsambas, 2006; Preskill & Donaldson, 2008).

The Role of Evaluation Capacity Building and Learning

> Learning is not attained by chance; it must be sought for with ardor and attended to with diligence.
>
> —Abigail Adams

Given the complicated and complex nature of the settings in which environmental evaluators work, and the comments made by several authors about the need for individual and organizational learning (e.g., Hildén, Chapter 1; Hockings et al., Chapter 5), it would seem that increased efforts to build the evaluation capacity of professionals in this arena make sense. Evaluation capacity building (ECB) has been a widely discussed topic in journal articles and presentations made at the American Evaluation Association annual conference over the last several years. On the basis of their recent research, Preskill and Boyle (2008) offer this definition of ECB:

> Evaluation capacity building involves the design and implementation of teaching and learning strategies to help individuals, groups, and organizations learn about what constitutes effective, useful, and professional evaluation practice. The ultimate goal of evaluation capacity building is sustainable evaluation practice—where members continuously ask questions that matter, collect, analyze, and interpret data, and use evaluation findings for decision-making and action. For evaluation practice to be sustained, participants must be provided with leadership support, incentives, resources, and opportunities to transfer their learning about evaluation to their everyday work. Sustainable evaluation practice also requires the development of systems, processes, policies, and plans that help embed evaluation work into the way the organization accomplishes its strategic mission and goals.

Preskill and Boyle view the outcome of ECB as sustainable evaluation practice. In addition, they place capacity building strategies and efforts within an organizational learning context. A key characteristic of capacity building is its intentionality of learning; thus it is not left to chance (Harnar & Preskill, 2007). From their review of the literature, Preskill and Boyle (2008) identified 10 teaching and learning strategies that could be used to help evaluators and practitioners learn from and about evaluation: participating in an evaluation process, training, technical assistance, mentoring and coaching, written materials, technologies, internships, meetings, Appreciative Inquiry, and communities of practice.

Interestingly, a few of the authors discussed, in some way, the value of developing networks or communities of practice (CoP) among evaluators and grantees as a means of sharing and learning from each other. As Bruyninckx (Chapter 3) suggests, "evaluators will have to set up flexible networks for generating knowledge and applying methods that can impart the necessary combination of professional expertise and skill." The suggestion by Kennedy et al. in Chapter 4 for developing networks "to link data uses and data providers" might be a potential community of practice. A network would be the means for people to come together who are engaged in similar kinds of evaluation. A community of practice, though often informal in structure, is more planned in terms of a meeting's focus—what participants want to learn, achieve, or share with each other. Participants in a CoP come together to share a concern or a passion for something they do and learn how to do it better as they interact regularly (Wenger, McDermott, & Snyder, 2002). Networks and communities of practice could meet face-to-face at summits, annual meetings, conferences, and other planned events. In addition, they could meet virtually through various collaborative learning technologies (e.g., www.intronetworks.com, www.huddle.net, www.basecamphq.com). My hope is that these networks and communities of practice could begin engaging in dialogue around the challenges mentioned in these chapters. Through participants' sharing of questions, ideas, and lessons learned, I believe great strides could be made in mediating some of the persistent dilemmas while further enhancing the effectiveness and utility of environmental evaluations.

Hope for Momentum

I greatly admire those who are working hard to offer meaningful and useful environmentally focused evaluations. Those who design and implement environmental programs and make environmental policies are vitally important to our future. There is no question that there will be difficult decisions to make in the very near future, and the answers to those questions may determine the quality of life for all species on this planet. Environmental evaluators have a critically important role in this endeavor, and I hope that this *NDE* generates both a momentum and a venue for continuing the conversation and for taking action. As the opening epigraph from Chief Seattle suggests, we are all connected; the future of one is the future of us all.

References

Eoyang, G. H. (2006). Human systems dynamics: Complexity-based approach to a complex evaluation. In B. Williams & I. Imam (Eds.), *Systems concepts in evaluation: An expert anthology* (pp. 123–140). Sconticut, MA: American Evaluation Association.

Frechtling, J. A. (2007). *Logic modeling methods in program evaluation*. San Francisco: Jossey-Bass.

Harnar, M., & Presskill, H. (2007). Evaluators' descriptions of process use: An exploratory study. *New Directions for Evaluation, 116*, 27–44.

Harnar, M., & Presskill, H. (2008). Evaluator's descriptions of process use: An exploratory study. *New Directions for Evaluation, 116*, 27–44.

Imam, I., LaGoy, A., & Williams, B. (2007). Introduction. In B. Williams & I. Imam (Eds.), *Systems concepts in evaluation: An expert anthology* (pp. 3–10). Sconticut, MA: American Evaluation Association.

Johnson, N. (2007). *Two's company, three is complexity*. Oxford: One World.

Kramer, M., Graves, R., Hirschhorn, J., & Fiske, L. (2007). *From insight to action: New directions in foundation evaluation*. Boston: FSG Social Impact Advisors.

Preskill, H., & Boyle, S. (2008). A conceptual model of evaluation capacity building: A Multidisciplinary perspective. *American Journal of Evaluation, 29*(4).

Preskill, H., & Catsambas, T. (2006). *Reframing evaluation through appreciative inquiry*. Thousand Oaks, CA: Sage.

Preskill, H., & Donaldson, S. I. (2008). Improving the evidence base for career development programs: Making use of the evaluation profession and positive psychology movement. *Advances in Human Resource Development, 10*(1), 104–121.

Snibbe, A. C. (2006, Fall). Drowning in data. *Stanford Social Innovation Review*, 39–45.

Wenger, E., McDermott, R., & Snyder, W. M. (2002). *Cultivating communities of practice*. Boston: Harvard Business School Press.

Woodwell, W. H., Jr. (2005). *Evaluation as a pathway to learning*. Washington, DC: Grantmakers for Effective Organizations.

HALLIE PRESKILL *is the director of strategic learning and evaluation at FSG Social Impact Advisors, a nonprofit organization that works with foundations, corporations, governments, and nonprofits to accelerate the pace of social progress.*

Mickwitz, P., & Birnbaum, M. (2009). Key insights for the design of environmental evaluations. In M. Birnbaum & P. Mickwitz (Eds.), *Environmental program and policy evaluation: Addressing methodological challenges. New Directions for Evaluation, 122*, 105–112.

10

Key Insights for the Design of Environmental Evaluations

Per Mickwitz, Matthew Birnbaum

Abstract

*Improving the future quality of program and policy evaluation in the environmental arena requires addressing four issues that emerged on reading the earlier chapters in this special issue. **Framing** the evaluation requires careful consideration in choosing the focus, and specifying the context and potentially confounding factors. It means identifying the purpose of the evaluation and the stakeholders most important for inclusion. Addressing **attribution** requires recognizing the limits of establishing causality while maintaining counterfactual thinking. More effort is needed to increase the **usefulness of evaluations**. Multiple stakeholders come with their own perspectives; addressing this heterogeneity requires transparency and feedback during the design, implementation, and follow-up to any evaluation study. Finally, improving the future quality of environmental evaluation will require continued **deliberation and community building**. Much of this is already underway, but the pluralism should still be promoted, and our community enlarged. Evaluators in the environmental field further should continue to be mindful of contributions coming from other subfields of evaluation and applied research beyond the environmental community.* © Wiley Periodicals, Inc.

Our view is that improving the quality of evaluation in the environmental field requires commitment to pluralism. Recognizing that there is not just one justified way to address any of the specific methodological challenges, we consciously designed this issue to comprise two chapters for each of four themes: time horizons, scaling, data credibility, and research designs and counterfactuals.

In this chapter, we do not review the four methodological challenges; these challenges are well covered in their respective sections. Instead, we want to use this concluding chapter to share what we believe are important insights into environmental evaluation that emerged from our discussions with the authors of this issue. Specifically, we address four issues that we consider crucial for the future of environmental program and policy evaluation: (1) framing of evaluations, (2) attribution in complex systems, (3) usefulness of evaluations, and (4) community and deliberation.

Framing Environmental Evaluations

As scientists know, the answers you get depend on the questions you ask; framing of evaluations is essential. Because environmental evaluations are typically undertaken for policies and programs addressing complex systems (Mickwitz & Birnbaum, Editors' Notes), determining the focus of an evaluation is neither easy nor straightforward. Environmental policies and programs are needed to mitigate the stress on the environment caused by human activities. Evaluations should therefore place increased emphasis on the linkages between policies and programs and the behavior of humans, individually as well as collectively (e.g., firms).

A key aspect of framing an evaluation is deciding what to evaluate and what to consider as context. The chapters of this issue give many examples of this. Bruyninckx (Chapter 3) and Hildén (Chapter 1) focus on public policies. Pullin and Knight (Chapter 6) focuses on specific conservation actions. The others focus on projects and programs. However, even within these broad categories, there are numerous options. One could focus on a specific policy instrument (e.g., a waste law), an aspect of such an instrument (e.g., a specific ban or requirement it contains), or on a bundle of instruments. Those aspects not put in the focus of an evaluation still need to be taken into account as potentially essential features of the context or possible confounding factors.

Another important aspect of framing an evaluation involves decisions about which scales matter and the relevant levels within each scale. As Bruyninckx (Chapter 3) points out, one needs to determine at what level of the social scale to focus the evaluation: local, national, or international. The social scale is broader than just the relevant public authorities addressing environmental issues. NGOs (especially those that are multinational in scope) and businesses operate on social scales that differ from those of public bodies. These actors' efforts should thus be evaluated and can consequently either be the focus of evaluations—in which case the public efforts naturally become part of the context—or they could be important confounding factors for evaluations of any public policy or program. This is critical because the levels along social scales frequently contrast with those of an environmental scale (e.g., a watershed transcending the boundaries of several states).

Effective framing of evaluations requires appropriate attention to timing—determining both when to do an evaluation and how to bound the time period being evaluated. Timing is especially crucial because environmental issues tend to have long time horizons and nonlinear effects and often are recursive in repeating themselves (Hildén, Chapter 1). At a minimum, evaluators need to explicitly adopt these realities into their evaluation design. Hildén, however, goes a step further in arguing for adopting evaluation approaches that consider different scenarios in connecting the past to the present and future. Evaluators who take the temporal aspect seriously need to frame their evaluations so that they can test competing theories of change. In doing so, they must account not only for initial impacts but also lagged effects. There are times when the anticipation of a policy shift causes a greater impact than its actual implementation. Further, the frequently nonlinear discontinuities of environmental change almost always dictate a difference in magnitude between long-term and short-term impacts.

The proper framing of an evaluation must also account for costs. Hockings et al. (Chapter 5) are concerned with the long-term persistence of the monitoring and evaluation designs, particularly for sophisticated quantitative designs that may not be sustainable over the long run. Ferraro (Chapter 7), on the other hand, argues that costs for more rigorous designs to assess counterfactuals may not be so great compared to the costs of environmental monitoring. In addition, one needs to account for the scenario where no funds are committed for evaluation and cost may occur because of missed opportunities for learning.

Framing an evaluation also implies determining the purpose of the evaluation and which stakeholders to involve (Preskill, Chapter 9). Determining the stakeholder in environmental issues is often challenging. Many groups are typically connected, either directly or indirectly, through environmental processes, material flows, or economic processes. Still, not everyone can be involved; too frequently breadth is chosen over depth. Tradeoffs inevitably arise between the evaluators' time and resources to analyze collected material and take into account expressed views on the one hand and the broad involvement of different stakeholders who can potentially raise important views and become adequately engaged on the other hand.

Program theories (or intervention theories or logic models, in the vocabulary of some of the authors) are excellent tools for focusing evaluations with respect to scale, timing, and stakeholders (Mickwitz, 2003).

But as stressed by Hildén (Chapter 1) and Weiss (2000) before him, it is important to use several alternative theories of change instead of just one, which likely would limit the perspective too much from the start.

Attribution Within Complex Systems

Policy and program evaluation in the environmental arena is confounded by the complexity of the systems in which these practitioners practice their craft. The basic theory of change starts with a strategy (set of actions) seeking to mitigate some human behavior (e.g., fertilizer use in agriculture leading to run-off of pollutants into streams), which stresses an environmental system (loss of oxygen in a stream). The consequences of the stress subsequently cause problems to the structure and function of the system (loss of a chain of interrelated species connected to the same water basin). The environmental community has historically focused on monitoring the natural characteristics of a system. Evaluation of policy and program interventions has recently emerged as a new focus thanks to the increased demands of public and private funders for greater accountability as well as practitioner interest in "adaptive management."

Black-box problems occur when one cannot identify the specific causes for observed outcomes (see Mickwitz & Birnbaum, Editors' Notes). These problems are real for evaluators working in this field. Even when additional resources are available for monitoring the impact of interventions on human behavior (e.g., bycatch of dolphins during commercial fishing practices), the question often remains unanswered as to whether the intervention will have its desired effect on the ecosystem (recovery of the dolphins). More to the point, it is rare for any one intervention to be discrete. Frequently, there are a multitude of interventions taking place simultaneously (as with education outreach to fishermen, labeling of dolphin-free fish products, incentives to fishermen to use alternative fishing gear, and regulations such as rules on bycatch). Even with sophisticated experimental designs, deciphering what causes what is extremely difficult to tease out if multiple interventions are simultaneously at play. Thus attribution at best is limited to testing bundles of interventions, which may have limited utility for generalizing to other circumstances. Improving the generalizability is a big factor for evaluation in this field, as the community moves from reviewing individual studies to synthesizing findings across multiple evaluations addressing similar contexts, strategies, and outcomes (Pullin & Knight, Chapter 6).

Despite limits to attribution, evaluation is not necessarily a doomed exercise. One strategy is "counterfactual thinking" (Ferraro, Chapter 7). In setting up theories of change, accounting for rival explanations becomes critical given the high level of uncertainty and lack of scientific knowledge often at play. This is especially true given the mismatch of skills in the environmental arena in which the dominant actors remain those trained in the natural sciences, who are frequently badly prepared to model the nuances of efforts to change human behavior. As a result, theories of change tend to be incomplete because the natural scientists are not well equipped to consider alternative theories of change or confounding variables that may affect human behavior.

While thinking systematically, evaluators are best off working incrementally to adopt to new changes of information—what Hildén (Chapter 1) calls "adaptive evaluation." Doing so raises sensitivity to resource constraints. We can guide deeper deliberation of what evidence exists about attribution through counterfactual thinking and triangulation of qualitative and quantitative data, methods, and perspectives (see Hockings et al., Chapter 5; and Margoluis, Stem, Salafsky, & Brown, in Chapter 8).

We acknowledge the limits on how far evaluators working in the environmental field will be able to test causal models given the real-world constraints described here. However, we are also cognizant of cultural shifts. The environmental arena for evaluation is one in which a cultural shift is needed to alter the focus to what works and does not work with policies and programs. It is no longer adequate to look only at natural actions leading to changes in environmental states in engaging in adaptive management; we have also reached the point where we need to focus on intermediary outcomes addressing human behaviors. This requires bringing in people with skills and experience in social sciences, especially in evaluation, and not simply shifting the job responsibilities of those trained in the natural sciences. Margoluis, Stem, and colleagues in Chapter 8 make this same point. As elaborated by Bruyninckx (Chapter 3), this commitment to evaluation in the environmental field frequently requires networking of interdisciplinary experts.

Facilitating Useful Environmental Evaluations

As stated by Michael Patton (1997, p. 20; emphasis in the original), ". . . evaluations should be judged by their utility and actual use; therefore, evaluators should facilitate the evaluation process and design any evaluation with careful consideration of how everything that is done *from beginning to end,* will affect use." Use may involve instrumental change to a decision or a conceptual alteration in how people conceive of an issue (Weiss & Bucuvalas, 1980). Even though enhancing the use of evaluations is necessary, it is not problem-free. The wide set of stakeholders, in relation to any environmental issue, may result in such broad involvement that nobody fully buys into the evaluation; the focus gets blurred and use becomes hindered. Unfortunately, we have seen this happen too often in the environmental field. But still, evaluation approaches without any involvement of key stakeholders with contesting claims, interests, and beliefs are far more problematic (Weiss, 1995). Promoting utilization of evaluations requires greater transparency of the evaluation results as well as the evaluation process and the methods used.

Wide involvement of stakeholders might be beneficial for the evaluation, especially for changing a culture of distrust and adversity to one of transparency and collaboration. However, accomplishing this goal requires careful determination of what roles are played with whom over the lifecycle of an evaluation. Not everyone wants or needs to be involved in every phase.

There are high expectations for evaluations that produce definitive answers and instrumental information for pressing but complex problems such as biodiversity conservation, climate change, and environmental risks of new technologies (such as genetically modified organisms or nanotechnologies). These expectations are likely to also result in disappointment, because even carefully designed evaluations of programs and policies addressing these "wicked problems" can seldom produce such certain or instrumental information. Frequently, the process of evaluation instead produces information that would have caused us to frame the evaluation differently had it been available in advance. Although such knowledge certainly may promote learning, it would be of a different kind than commonly expected. Evaluators and those commissioning environmental evaluations will have to discuss the nature of both knowledge production and use in order to handle these likely disappointments constructively.

In her commentary to this volume, Preskill (Chapter 9) wrote that she "can't help wondering if this deductive and problem-focused approach might not actually limit our creativity, innovation, and understanding of the process and impact of environmental programs and their evaluations." We see three possibilities for supplying a positive message to users that will not result in dogma and inaction but, we hope, result rather in creativity and innovation. First, evaluations may produce knowledge showing that environmental policies and programs can make a difference. The second possibility to focus on opportunities instead of threats and limits is to use the concept of "ecosystem services" (e.g., oyster beds functioning to filter water quality), emphasizing the positive values from these multitude of services as "ecological assets." Third, even though environmental problems, such as climate change, framed as problems produce images of costs and restrictions, they can be reframed as sustainable energy production that may generate a picture of innovation, business opportunity, profit, and desired social change. In the case of climate change, such a reframing is actually taking place in many countries to such a degree that it may be hiding the tradeoffs and conflicts that also exist. Reframing problems as opportunities can hugely affect what kind of policies, programs, and projects gets started. It is then up to the evaluations to determine whether these interventions are effective, taking both desired and undesired effects into account.

Furthering Deliberation and Building Community

As many of the authors note in their chapters, evaluation came rather late to the environmental field. Surely one can find older examples, but to a large extent retrospective environmental evaluation of policies, programs, and projects has a history of only about a decade. Prior evaluations were typically very ad hoc. There was no Environmental Topical Interest Group (TIG) in AEA and hardly any articles related to evaluation published in the American or European evaluation journals. Today many of the questions addressed by the environmental evaluators are still the same as a decade ago. Many of the methodological challenges faced are still the same and still appear at least as big. Yet the current situation is fundamentally different because a community has been built in recent years. The extent and depth of this community is evidenced by the chapters in this special issue. This issue became possible through the emergence of an active community. This community has most clearly manifested in the Environmental Evaluators Networking Forum annual gathering in Washington, D.C.[1] The community has at its base a diverse set of actors who have come to the environmental evaluation field. Some come with a background in evaluation but are new to the environmental field. Many are practitioners with skills in the environment as social (or more likely natural) scientists but are unaware of the larger evaluation literature. This issue of NDE is a response to explicit demands by this community. It is also a product of the deliberations of this community. How the insights here will be transferred into practice and further developed largely depends on the continued deliberation within this community of evaluators.

Evaluations of environmental policies and programs will continue to be evaluations of a complex mix of measures addressing complex environmental issues. The problems are of great magnitude, be they dealing with climate change or increasing ecosystem resilience. The community of evaluators in the environmental field will thus have to expand to encompass an even larger set of academics, public servants, private consultants, and representatives of foundations and nonprofit organizations. We need more voices examining not just particular evaluations but also the stream of those surfacing. If the natural scientists are right, environmental problems are only going to become more visible and complex, dominating day-to-day realities for both humans and wildlife. If we can improve our framing of evaluations, increase the rigor of counterfactual thinking within complex systems, make our evaluations more useful, and enable deeper deliberation, then we will have a better chance of addressing these pressing problems and ensuring the future well-being of humans as well as nature.

Note

1. For more information about the Environmental Evaluators Network, see http://www.nfwf.org/AM/Template.cfm?Section=Enviromental_Evaluators_Network.

Another network that has emerged over the past decade is the Conservation Measures Partnership (CMP), which includes many of the large American-based multinational conservation organizations. For more information about CMP, see www.conservation measures.org/CMP.

References

Conservation Measures Partnership. (2007). *Open standards for the practice of conservation.* Version 2.0. Available at http://conservationmeasures.org/CMP/Site_Docs/CMP_Open_Standards_Version_2.0.pdf

Mickwitz, P. (2003). A framework for evaluating environmental policy instruments: Context and key concepts. *Evaluation, 9*(4), 415–436.

Patton, M. Q. (1997). *Utilization-focused evaluation: The new century text* (3rd ed.). London: Sage.

Weiss, C. (2000). Which links in which theories shall we evaluate? In P. J. Rogers, T. A. Hacsi, A. Petrosino, & T. A. Huebner (Eds.), Program theory in evaluation: Challenges and opportunities. *New Directions for Evaluation, 87,* 35–45. San Francisco: Jossey-Bass.

Weiss, C. H. (1995). The four "I's" of school reform: How interests, ideology, information, and institution affect teachers and principals. *Harvard Educational Review, 65*(4), 571–592.

Weiss, C. H., & Bucuvalas, M. (1980, April). Truth test and utility test: Decision makers' frame of reference for social science research. *American Sociological Review,* 302–313.

PER MICKWITZ works as a senior researcher at the Research Programme for Environmental Policy at the Finnish Environment Institute. He is also an adjunct professor of environmental policy at the University of Tampere.

MATTHEW BIRNBAUM has been working as an evaluation officer at the National Fish and Wildlife Foundation and in that capacity is a cofounder of the Environmental Evaluators Network; he is also affiliated with American University as an adjunct professor.

INDEX

ORDER FORM SUBSCRIPTION AND SINGLE ISSUES

DISCOUNTED BACK ISSUES:

Use this form to receive 20% off all back issues of *New Directions for Evaluation.*
All single issues priced at **$23.20** (normally $29.00)

TITLE	ISSUE NO.	ISBN

Call 888-378-2537 or see mailing instructions below. When calling, mention the promotional code JB9ND to receive your discount. For a complete list of issues, please visit www.josseybass.com/go/ev

SUBSCRIPTIONS: (1 YEAR, 4 ISSUES)

☐ New Order   ☐ Renewal

U.S.	☐ Individual: $85	☐ Institutional: $235
CANADA/MEXICO	☐ Individual: $85	☐ Institutional: $275
ALL OTHERS	☐ Individual: $109	☐ Institutional: $309

Call 888-378-2537 or see mailing and pricing instructions below.
Online subscriptions are available at www.interscience.wiley.com

ORDER TOTALS:

Issue / Subscription Amount: $ _____

Shipping Amount: $ _____
(for single issues only – subscription prices include shipping)

Total Amount: $ _____

SHIPPING CHARGES:	
First Item	$5.00
Each Add'l Item	$3.00

(No sales tax for U.S. subscriptions. Canadian residents, add GST for subscription orders. Individual rate subscriptions must be paid by personal check or credit card. Individual rate subscriptions may not be resold as library copies.)

BILLING & SHIPPING INFORMATION:

☐ **PAYMENT ENCLOSED:** *(U.S. check or money order only. All payments must be in U.S. dollars.)*

☐ **CREDIT CARD:**   ☐ VISA   ☐ MC   ☐ AMEX

Card number _____ Exp. Date_____

Card Holder Name_____ Card Issue # _____

Signature _____ Day Phone_____

☐ **BILL ME:** *(U.S. institutional orders only. Purchase order required.)*

Purchase order # _____
Federal Tax ID 13559302 • GST 89102-8052

Name_____

Address_____

Phone_____ E-mail_____

Copy or detach page and send to: **John Wiley & Sons, PTSC, 5th Floor**
                                    989 Market Street, San Francisco, CA 94103-1741

Order Form can also be faxed to: **888-481-2665**

PROMO JB9ND

JB JOSSEY-BASS™

▶ New and Noteworthy Titles in **Research Methods**

Research Essentials: An Introduction to Designs and Practices,
Stephen D. Lapan (Editor), MaryLynn T. Quartaroli (Editor), ISBN:
9780470181096, Paperback, 384 pages, 2009, $75.00.

Research Methods for Everyday Life: Blending Qualitative and
Quantitative Approaches
Scott W. VanderStoep, Deidre D. Johnson, ISBN: 9780470343531,
Paperback, 352 pages, 2009. $75.00.

Methods in Educational Research: From Theory to Practice
Marguerite G. Lodico, Dean T. Spaulding, Katherine H. Voegtle, ISBN:
9780787979621, Hardcover, 440 pages, April 2006, $75.00.

SPSS Essentials: Managing and Analyzing Social Sciences Data
John T. Kulas, ISBN: 9780470226179, Paperback, 272 pages, 2008, $45.00.

Quantitative Data Analysis: Doing Social Research to Test Ideas
Donald J. Treiman, ISBN: 9780470380031, Paperback, 480 pages, 2009.
$75.00.

Mixed Methods in Social Inquiry
Jennifer C. Greene, ISBN: 9780787983826, Paperback, 232 pages, 2007,
$45.00.

Action Research Essentials
Dorothy Valcarel Craig, ISBN: 9780470189290, Paperback, 272 pages, 2009.
$45.00.

Designing and Constructing Instruments for Social Research and
Evaluation
David Colton, Robert W. Covert, ISBN: 9780787987848, Paperback, 412
pages, 2007, $55.00.

AEA members: Take advantage of your 20 percent discount on these
titles by ordering at (877) 762-2974 or www.josseybass.com or and
entering code AEAF9.

JB JOSSEY-BASS™

▶ New and Noteworthy Titles in **Evaluation**

Program Evaluation in Practice: Core Concepts and Examples for
Discussion and Analysis
Dean T. Spaulding, ISBN: 9780787986858, Paperback, 176 pages, 2008,
$40.00

Evaluation Essentials: Methods For Conducting Sound Research
Beth Osborne Daponte, ISBN: 9780787984397, Paperback, 192 pages, 2008,
$60.00.

Evaluation Theory, Models, and Applications
Daniel L. Stufflebeam, Anthony J. Shinkfield, ISBN: 9780787977658,
Hardcover, 768 pages, 2007, $70.00.

Logic Modeling Methods in Program Evaluation
Joy A. Frechtling, ISBN: 9780787981969, Paperback, 160 pages, 2007,
$48.00.

Evaluator Competencies: Standards for the Practice of Evaluation in
Organizations
Darlene F. Russ-Eft, Marcie J. Bober, Ileana de la Teja, Marguerite Foxon,
Tiffany A. Koszalka, ISBN: 9780787995997, Hardcover, 240 pages, 2008,
$50.00

Youth Participatory Evaluation: Strategies for Engaging Young People
Kim Sabo Flores, ISBN: 9780787983925, Paperback, 208 pages, 2007, $45.00

Performance Evaluation: Proven Approaches for Improving Program
and Organizational Performance
Ingrid J. Guerra-López, ISBN: 9780787988838, Paperback, 320 pages, 2008,
$45.00

AEA members: Take advantage of your 20 percent discount on these
titles by ordering at (877) 762-2974 or www.josseybass.com or and
entering code AEAF9.

Why Wait to Make Great Discoveries

When you can make them in an instant with Wiley InterScience® Pay-Per-View and ArticleSelect™

Now you can have instant, full-text access to an extensive collection of journal articles or book chapters available on Wiley InterScience. With Pay-Per-View and ArticleSelect™, there's no limit to what you can discover...

ArticleSelect™ is a token-based service, providing access to full-text content from non-subscribed journals to existing institutional customers (EAL and BAL)

Pay-per-view is available to any user, regardless of whether they hold a subscription with Wiley InterScience.

Benefits:

- Access online full-text content from journals and books that are outside your current library holdings
- Use it at home, on the road, from anywhere at any time
- Build an archive of articles and chapters targeted for your unique research needs
- Take advantage of our free profiled alerting service the perfect companion to help you find specific articles in your field as soon as they're published
- Get what you need instantly no waiting for document delivery
- Fast, easy, and secure online credit card processing for pay-per-view downloads
- Special, cost-savings for EAL customers: whenever a customer spends tokens on a title equaling 115% of its subscription price, the customer is auto-subscribed for the year
- Access is instant and available for 24 hours

⊕WILEY
InterScience®
DISCOVER SOMETHING GREAT

www.interscience.wiley.com